The Atlanta Journal-Constitution

DawgNation

GLORY, GLORY

The GEORGIA BULLDOGS Repeat as National Champions

Hyosub Shin/The Atlanta Journal-Constitution

SPECIAL COMMEMORATIVE EDITION

The Atlanta Journal-Constitution

A COX ENTERPRISES COMPANY

Andrew Morse, President and Publisher
Bala Sundaramoorthy, Vice President and General Manager
Kevin G. Riley, Editor
Mark A. Waligore, Managing Editor
Shawn McIntosh, Managing Editor
Leroy Chapman Jr., Managing Editor
Zachary McGhee, Senior Director, Digital Audience Experience
Chris Vivlamore, Sports Editor
Leo Willingham, Book Editor
Sandra Brown, Visuals Editor
Brandon Adams, Bob Andres, Mark Bradley, Gabriel Burns, Curtis Compton, Michael Cunningham,
Steve Hummer, Jason Getz, Mike Griffith, Connor Riley, Doug Roberson, Hyosub Shin, Ken Sugiura,
Chip Towers, Barbara Vivlamore, David Wellham, Contributors

This book is available in quantity at special discounts for your group or organization.
For further information, contact:

Triumph Books LLC
814 North Franklin Street
Chicago, Illinois 60610
Phone: (312) 337-0747
www.triumphbooks.com

Printed in U.S.A.
ISBN: 978-1-63727-483-5

Content packaged by Mojo Media, Inc.
Joe Funk: Editor
Jason Hinman: Creative Director

Front cover photo by Jason Getz/The Atlanta Journal-Constitution
Back cover photo by Hyosub Shin/The Atlanta Journal-Constitution

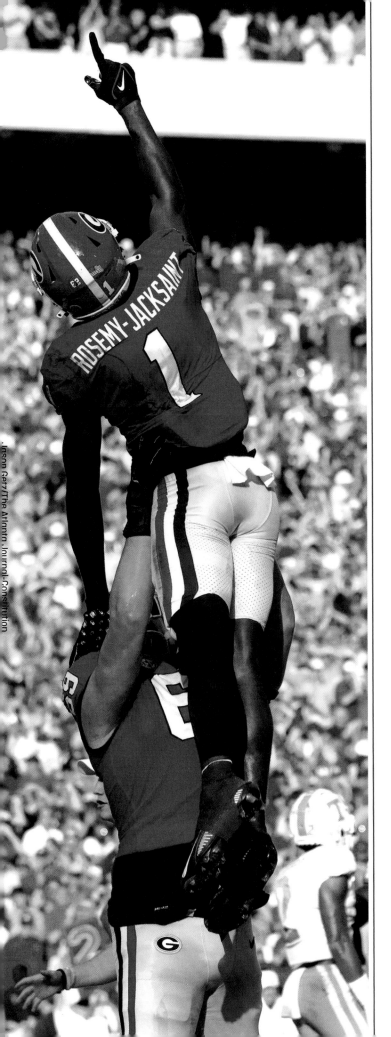

Jason Getz/The Atlanta Journal-Constitution

CONTENTS

FOREWORD

The Perfect Season

By Scott Woerner

I cannot imagine that any University of Georgia football player who has ever put on that red helmet has not dreamed of making "the play." You know, the winning play, the play that decides the game, the play that ends any threat of blemish to an undefeated season. They all dream of The Perfect Season.

Those of us who played on Georgia's championship team of 1980 had that type of attitude. That was the last perfect season for the Bulldogs, though I'd say it was probably more magical than perfect. Every Saturday, it seemed, a teammate would step up with a great play in one facet of the game or another.

The memories of the great plays from the '80s echo in the calls of the late, great Larry Munson: on offense ("There goes Herschel!"), on defense ("I know I'm asking a lot, you guys, but hunker it down one more time!") or on special teams ("He's at the 45, the 40, the 35 ...!"). Sometimes it was a fantastic play that can only be described as a miracle ("Lindsay Scott, Lindsay Scott, Lindsay Scott!").

I had several discussions over the years with our coach, Vince Dooley, who died at the age of 90 in late October. Attempting to define the perfection that occurred 42 years ago, he liked the description of "miraculous." We just always found a way to win. Half of our victories came by a touchdown or less.

"Miraculous" does not apply to these Kirby Smart-coached Bulldogs. "Dominant" is the word that best suits them. They entered the College Football Playoff winning games by an average margin of nearly 27 points. From there, it was the pursuit of

perfection. The players' memories from that incredible championship run in 2021 had a pesky "1" in the loss column, nagging them like a hangnail. No such flaw could discolor the 2022 season.

The similarity in all great Georgia teams over the years is stifling, smothering, stingy defense. Legendary defensive coordinator Erk Russell set the bar high, and Smart's teams keep clearing it. Coach Russell had many sayings, but one that was special to all his defensive charges was posted prominently on the wall in the hall of the Coliseum, and we passed it daily:

> *If we score, we may win.*
> *If they score, we may lose.*
> *If they never score, we will never lose.*

The 2022 defense certainly exhibited that attitude, game after game, all season long. They kept high quality teams out of the end zone. From a defensive player's point of view, it was a pleasure to watch what might be the best defensive group ever assembled at the University of Georgia.

The quality went two and three players deep at every position, and all of them got to see playing time. The teams of 1980-82 also were loaded with talent. In the 17-10 Sugar Bowl victory against Notre Dame, every member of the defense played that night and contributed to the win.

Football truly is a team sport, the greatest team sport. Yet there always are special players on every winning team. The 2022 national champions had

Hyosub Shin/The Atlanta Journal-Constitution

their share of exceptional players. Several were All-Americans, but more important, they were "team" over "me" players.

Stop and listen to the boys throwing the ball in the quad during tailgates, or on playgrounds at elementary schools, and you will hear their names being called. "I'm gonna be Stetson Bennett" or "I want to be Brock Bowers," the boys shout as their games begin. McIntosh, McConkey and Milton, they're all familiar names now. This next generation of Bulldogs will want to lift each in the air with one hand while holding up the No. 1 finger on their other, à la Jalen Carter in the SEC Championship game victory over LSU. What a moment!

It helps that all these games are now on television. In our day, we were lucky to be on TV once or twice a season. But then we were fortunate to have the legendary Munson calling out our names on the radio. Listening to him made you feel you had a ticket to the game.

Bennett has garnered a lot of attention because of his circuitous route from walk-on to junior college, to Heisman Trophy candidate and quarterback of back-to-back national champions. Likewise, the 1980 team had a bunch of former walk-ons. Robert Miles, Nate Taylor, Mike Fisher, Dale Williams, Bob Kelly, Jim Broadway, Mark Malkiewicz and George Kesler all paid their dues before donning the "G" in a game.

Championships don't just happen. They require hard work, senior leadership, self-sacrifice, perseverance and discipline from the players. They require dedicated, savvy coaches who know how to put you in position to win. And, yes, they require some luck.

Winning one championship is difficult, but repeating is a nearly impossible task. This team repeated. They did so because they have one of the greatest coaches of our time in Kirby Smart. But everyone at the University of Georgia, from President Jere Morehead all the way down to the people who mow the grass on what is now Dooley Field can share with great pride what it is like to be a national champion.

Go Dawgs!

INTRODUCTION

By Mark Bradley

W in once, and you're a champion – and that's nice. Win again, and you're historic. As they say in baseball, flags fly forever. Two flags, claimed in consecutive seasons, plop a team atop its own mountain. We'll call Georgia's peak Mt. Kirby.

Hired from Alabama to make Georgia win like Alabama, Kirby Paul Smart has done the deed. He recruited like crazy. He coached like a Saban, like a Belichick, like a Krzyzewski. He went 29-1 and claimed back-to-back titles with a quarterback who arrived as a walk-on. After beating Alabama for the title in January 2022, the Bulldogs lost five defenders in the first round of the NFL draft, the kind of exodus that would stunt any team's growth. Somehow Georgia grew stronger.

We'll argue forever which of these champions was better, but there's no question that the second edition was more clinical. Only twice over the two seasons did an opponent score 41 points against Georgia. The first time was in the 2021 SEC championship game. The Bulldogs lost by 17. The second came in the 2022 semifinal against Ohio State, a game so overstuffed it spilled into a second year. These Bulldogs won by a point.

Of the 29 victories over two seasons, that stands apart. Our final question was if Georgia could win a shootout. (It had proved, many times over, its worth in blowouts.) No knock on TCU, which the Bulldogs beat for the second title, but Ohio State was the one team that could approximate UGA's talent and skill. The Buckeyes led by 14 points in the second, third and fourth quarters. Georgia led for a total of 109 seconds. Timing is everything.

Georgia played its first collegiate football game in 1892. It has won four national championships. Half of those came these past two seasons, with Smart as coach, with Stetson Bennett as quarterback. We've heard tales of Sinkwich and Trippi. We've seen Herschel's highlights a thousand times. As glorious as those eras were, neither yielded two titles. Two in a row, having beaten Michigan and Alabama for the first, Ohio State and TCU for the second – that changes everything.

No longer do we ask if/when the Bulldogs can beat Bama. That happened. No longer need we wonder if Smart can take his program from strength to strength. That happened, too. Georgia has become Alabama. Georgia is the gold standard of college football. The history of the College Football Playoff isn't long, but no team had gone 4-0 in consecutive tournaments. This one just did.

Beyond that, words fail. We saw the Bulldogs lift one championship trophy in Indianapolis. They hoisted another in L.A. The greatest era of Georgia football? It's right here, right now. I'll shut up and let you enjoy it. ∎

GEORGIA 65, TCU 7

January 9, 2023 ● Inglewood, California

UNSTOPPABLE!

Georgia Bulldogs Cement Legend with Back-to-Back National Titles

By Chip Towers

"You've got nine days to become legendary."

That was Georgia coach Kirby Smart's message to his team in the postgame locker room following the Bulldogs' narrow 42-41 escape of Ohio State in the College Football Playoff semifinals at Mercedes-Benz Stadium.

Nine days and three time zones later, the Bulldogs are officially legends. They'll be remembered as one of the great teams of all-time.

After the 65-7 victory over TCU to claim the 2022 national championship, Smart and Stetson Bennett could stake a claim as Georgia's coach and player "GOATs" – Greatest Of All Time.

Smart wasn't willing to accept such a label for himself, but he fully endorsed it for his quarterback.

"I know he will have GOAT status in Georgia forever," Smart said. "And he should."

It was fitting, then, that Smart called a timeout early in the fourth quarter of the blowout win. He did it so that Bennett, a sixth-year senior, could receive an ovation. They met each other as Bennett walked toward the sideline and shared a long, emotional embrace.

"One last huddle," Bennett said. "As simple as that seems, that was special."

Said Smart, known for chewing out his star signal-caller: "(It was the) first time he's ever walked off the field and I hugged him."

They both laughed hard at that one.

With nearly an entire quarter left to play, Bennett already had accounted for six touchdowns, four with his arm and two with his legs. He left with 304 yards on 18-of-25 passing and 39 yards rushing on three carries. That makes him the first 4,000-yard quarterback in UGA history.

"I wouldn't have believed it (his story)," Bennett said, if somebody had told him how his college career would end. "I don't know, guess I'd say it's a good thing I signed with Georgia."

Both Smart, as coach, and Bennett, as quarterback, are the first in the College Football Playoff era to win back-to-back national football championships. Before that, Alabama was the last team to repeat as champion. Smart was defensive coordinator for the Crimson Tide when they repeated in 2012.

Legendary Georgia coach Vince Dooley, who died at the age of 90 on Oct. 28, could not do it despite fielding powerhouse teams in 1980 and '81. Likewise, no Georgia quarterback or player of any ilk

Wide receiver Ladd McConkey catches a 37-yard touchdown pass during the first quarter. (Hyosub Shin/The Atlanta Journal-Constitution)

has contributed to back-to-back titles. Buck Belue was unable to lead the Bulldogs back in 1981, and World War II prevented it in 1943.

The too-small walk-on from Blackshear, Bennett did what none of those others could do. Dismissed for two years as not being good enough to pilot a championship team, Bennett made every play that mattered the past two seasons while leading the Bulldogs to wins in 28 of their past 29 games.

As he leaves Georgia, there is no jealousy from teammates, only appreciation.

"I salute my boy," senior running back Kenny McIntosh said. "He did what he had to do. All those 'yeah, but' people that are always talking about him? Yeah, well, he won the championship twice. So there."

Fittingly, after Bennett went out, sophomore Carson Beck led the Bulldogs on another scoring drive. The final points gave the Bulldogs the largest margin of victory in a playoff championship game. Georgia would score again after that.

There were defensive legends produced as well. Count Javon Bullard among them. A sophomore defensive back from Milledgeville, Bullard atoned for an early defensive-holding penalty with a fumble recovery and two interceptions. His second pick set up Georgia's final score of the first half with 26 seconds remaining. The Bulldogs went to the halftime locker room leading 38-7, the largest first-half margin in playoff history.

"Obviously it snowballed on us," TCU coach Sonny Dykes said. "That hasn't happened to us before this year. We tried to figure a way back in it, and we couldn't do it. But proud of what our team did this year."

That Georgia won was no surprise. The No. 1-ranked Bulldogs (15-0) entered the final game as 12.5-point favorites over TCU, according to Las Vegas

In his final appearance for the Georgia Bulldogs, Stetson Bennett recorded 304 yards on 18-of-25 passing and 39 yards rushing on three carries. He left to an ovation early in the fourth quarter. (Jason Getz/ The Atlanta Journal-Constitution)

oddsmakers. That was the largest line in the era of the playoff, which began in 2014.

That's because the Horned Frogs (13-2) arrived at SoFi Stadium as the proverbial sports Cinderella. In their first year under Dykes, they were considered a 200-to-1 shot just to make the playoff this season and were picked to finish seventh in the Big 12. Meanwhile, Max Duggan didn't even begin the season as TCU's starting quarterback. He lost a preseason competition to Chandler Morris.

But Morris was injured in the season opener, Duggan took over midgame and became runner-up for the Heisman Trophy while leading the Frogs to an undefeated regular season. Counted out at every turn, No. 3 TCU was thought to be severely overmatched by Michigan in the semifinals. Yet it won in an exhilarating shootout, 51-45.

When it was over, there could have been track marks from a tank where the Bulldogs had run roughshod over the Frogs. Georgia had 539 yards of offense and had allowed TCU only eight first downs when Smart called off the Dogs. Duggan was sacked six times, while throwing for only 152 yards on 14-of-22 passing, with two interceptions.

As for Georgia, this was its third time in the playoff in seven seasons under Smart, and it made the championship game every time. The Bulldogs lost to Alabama in the 2017 season CFP final at Mercedes-Benz Stadium in Smart's second season, then vanquished the Tide and Smart's mentor, Nick Saban, 33-18 in Indianapolis last year.

The game was competitive only for the first quarter. It turned after a five-play, 75-yard TCU scoring drive trimmed Georgia's early lead to 10-7 with 4:45 remaining. But the Bulldogs answered with a four-play

Tight end Darnell Washington makes a reception over TCU safety Abraham Camara for a 28-yard gain in the third quarter. (Hyosub Shin/The Atlanta Journal-Constitution)

touchdown on three 11-yard plays followed by a 37-yard touchdown pass from Bennett to Ladd McConkey.

That Georgia accomplished that feat after losing 15 players from the '21 team to the NFL draft and another 13 to transfer portal will go down as one of the great coaching feats of all time. That Smart did so while also replacing four assistant coaches only adds to the legend.

Now a new challenge awaits Smart and the Bulldogs. They all fielded numerous questions about a "three-peat."

Smart didn't want to hear it.

"The biggest challenge is the same as we face in society – entitlement," Georgia's seventh-year coach said. "I personally think next year is going to be much more of a challenge. Last year, we had a bunch of guys leave. This team has a lot of guys coming back. The disease that comes into a young program is entitlement. We have to work like we worked for this one." ■

Above: Kirby Smart calls in a play during the second half. Opposite: Brock Bowers catches a 22-yard touchdown pass for a 45-7 Georgia lead in the third quarter. (Hyosub Shin/The Atlanta Journal-Constitution)

MAKING IT LOOK EASY

Bulldogs are Champions Again, But Don't Take It for Granted

By Michael Cunningham • January 9, 2023

Most Georgia fans at SoFi Stadium had trekked into the soggy Southern California night, satisfied after watching their Bulldogs bludgeon TCU, when Kirby Smart delivered a message for them.

"They can't take it for granted," Smart said. "You can't take opportunities like this for granted. They showed up in full force. They better never get tired of it because we need them here. We need them to back us.

"And you can't become complacent as a fan, and we can't become complacent as coaches."

Smart's audience should have no problem getting that message. For decades, Georgia was one of college football's great underachievers. Smart has helped to build the program into a dominant force, but it's not easy. The Bulldogs just made it look that way while beating TCU into submission with a national title on the line.

Georgia is the undefeated, unquestioned king of college football for the 2022 season after beating TCU 65-7 in the national championship game. The Bulldogs are the first back-to-back champions since Alabama in 2011-12.

Smart beat his old boss, Alabama coach Nick Saban, for last season's national title. Now he's one-upped Saban with a 15-0 season, matching Clemson (2018) and LSU (2019).

Oddsmakers had No. 1 Georgia favored by 13.5 points at kickoff. That's the largest point spread in a national championship game since college football started holding them in 1998. It turns out the betting markets badly underestimated the Bulldogs, who made third-ranked TCU look like Kent State.

That's not fair to the Flashes, who played Georgia tough for a half in September. The Horned Frogs had one competitive moment, getting their deficit down to 10-7 in the first quarter, before Georgia rolled to an easy victory. The victory was astonishing in its completeness.

Georgia quarterback Stetson Bennett was brilliant in his final college game. He passed for 304 yards with four touchdowns and ran for two more scores. Bennett took one snap in the fourth quarter before taking the rest of the night off.

"What he did was truly amazing," Smart said. "Probably had his best game of his career."

Ohio State embarrassed Georgia's great defense in the Peach Bowl. That group earned redemption by shutting down TCU's high-scoring offense.

Head coach Kirby Smart kisses the College Football Playoff National Championship Trophy after guiding the Georgia Bulldogs to their second consecutive title. (Hyosub Shin/The Atlanta Journal-Constitution)

"We had about a perfect night," Smith said.

To have a chance, the Horned Frogs needed to play great and catch Georgia on an off-night. Neither of those things happened. TCU's improbable, special run to the championship game ended with a humbling defeat to the nation's best team.

Before the game, ESPN asked TCU coach Sonny Dykes how his team could pull an upset.

"We believe we can, most importantly," Dykes said.

It didn't take long to see that Dykes was wrong. His players didn't really believe they could win. And who can blame them? Everyone could see that Georgia was too big, too fast and too good for TCU.

The Bulldogs scored every time they had the ball in the first half. By the time TCU finally stopped them, they led 38-7. The Bulldogs scored another touchdown when they got the ball back again, forced a three-and-out by TCU, and then scored another TD. More than 20 minutes remained in the game, but it was over.

The Bulldogs didn't just show they have a big edge over TCU in player talent. Georgia's coaches also outflanked their TCU counterparts. The Bulldogs were more focused and physical. Georgia escaped with a victory in the Peach Bowl after falling behind early. This time, the Bulldogs took the fight to TCU from the start and never relented.

Afterwards, the smell of cigar smoke filled the corridors around Georgia's locker room.

"This is what we do it for all year, for that moment in the locker room," Georgia's Kenny McIntosh said, while puffing on a cigar.

This was the crowning achievement of a new era of Georgia football. Last season's national championship wasn't a one-off. After falling short of expectations for so long, the Bulldogs are built to keep winning big for longer than they've ever done it.

Georgia had all-time great Herschel Walker for three years, won one national championship and then didn't play for another for nearly 40 years. The Bulldogs went 20 years between SEC titles. Conference rivals Florida, Auburn, LSU, Alabama and Tennessee had great teams win championships. Georgia Tech did it, too.

Georgia football was stuck on mediocre for a long time. Then former athletic director Greg McGarity hired Smart, who'd played for the Bulldogs. He took the job with the understanding that Georgia would pour money into the program, like Saban had done at Alabama. Smart got everything he wanted and, now, so has Georgia.

There was a time when it wasn't clear that would happen. Smart's Bulldogs played for a national championship in Year 2, losing to Alabama, and then didn't make it back to the CFP over the next three years. Smart erred in picking quarterback Jake Fromm over Justin Fields. As Alabama, LSU and Clemson won national titles with wide-open offensive attacks, Smart insisted that he wasn't stuck in his "man ball" ways of grinding out yards on the ground.

Smart first proved that by hiring Todd Monken, an ex-NFL coordinator, to modernize Georgia's offense. Monken helped make Bennett, the former walk-on, a bona fide star. The Bulldogs don't have the big-play threats at wide receiver like other title contenders. So, Monken fashioned an attack that emphasizes throwing passes to the perimeter and highlights talented tight end Brock Bowers.

Stetson Bennett celebrates at SoFi Stadium following Georgia's dominant 65-7 win over TCU for the national championship. (Hyosub Shin/The Atlanta Journal-Constitution)

The Horned Frogs had no chance to stop that formula. They had a plan to be aggressive on defense. Bennett and Monken took advantage of that eagerness. They had TCU's defenders going one way while the play went the other.

Bennett's 21-yard touchdown run was a beautiful display of deception, timing and precision. His fake handoff to Daijun Edwards was so convincing that TCU's entire defensive front shifted left. Bennett kept the ball and ran the other direction and scored without being touched. Another crafty run fake by Bennett fooled a defensive back who was supposed to be tracking Ladd McConkey. He was wide open to catch Bennett's 37-yard TD pass for a 14-7 lead.

After the Bulldogs turned a turnover into three points, it looked as if TCU might finally stop them on their next drive. Bennett kept them going. He sidestepped a blitzing defender and ran 11 yards to convert a third-and-10.

Said Smart: "He knew what was coming and he set the guy up."

Bennett ended that drive with a six-yard TD run, untouched again, for a 24-7 lead. Now the Bulldogs were rolling. TCU couldn't stop them. No one could beat them all season. Smart shouldn't worry that anyone associated with Georgia football will ever take it for granted. ∎

Georgia players and coach Kirby Smart celebrate the Bulldogs' national championship and perfect 15-0 season. (Hyosub Shin/The Atlanta Journal-Constitution)

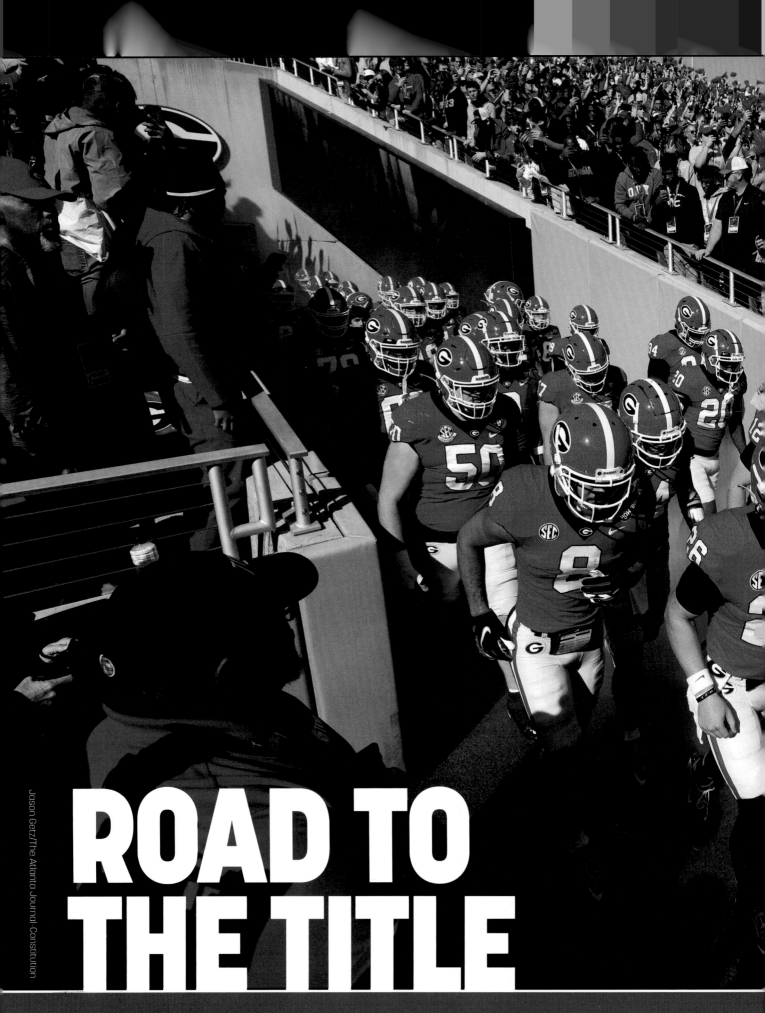

ROAD TO
THE TITLE

BUILT TO SUSTAIN

The Next Step for Kirby Smart and Georgia – Total Domination

By Mark Bradley • July 20, 2022

It was Nov. 16, 2002, a cold day at Auburn. On fourth-and-15 with 1:25 left, David Greene threw long for Michael Johnson, who outjumped Horace Willis, who didn't jump. On that day of deliverance, coach Mark Richt said his Bulldogs "knocked the lid off the Georgia program."

And they did, sort of. That famous play – 70-X-Takeoff – gained Georgia its first berth in an SEC Championship game, in which it annihilated Arkansas. After 20 years without a conference title, the Bulldogs were back in the high life. They again were nationally relevant.

And yet, try as he might, Richt couldn't make Georgia a national champion. He was fired after a 15-year tenure that was a success in every other way. In came alumnus Kirby Smart, who nearly won it all in his second season. But Tua Tagovailoa found DeVonta Smith on second-and-26. Everything went *ka-blooey* again.

Three seasons passed. Georgia under Smart never seemed less than one of the nation's 10 best teams – they were 31-7 over those three years – but they couldn't get past Alabama or, in 2019, the LSU that briefly became Alabama. Smart heard doubts from the louder quadrants of Bulldog Nation: He couldn't handle quarterbacks; he cared only about defense; he was too stubborn to change with the times.

With 8:30 remaining in 2022's national championship game, Georgia trailed Bama 18-13.

Then Stetson Bennett, who wasn't supposed to be good enough, found Adonai Mitchell deep. Then Bennett hit Brock Bowers in the left flat. Then Kelee Ringo intercepted Bryce Young's overthrown pass and ran it back. Over the final 8:29, the Bulldogs outscored Bama 20-0.

With that, the figurative lid had been obliterated. Georgia was national champion. It will be national champion again. There's no program better positioned to become the next Alabama, not even Bama itself.

Nick Saban turns 71 on Halloween 2022. It's possible to see him coaching another two or three seasons. It is not possible to envision him coaching beyond 75. Smart, by way of contrast, won't turn 50 until Dec. 23, 2025.

Georgia saw five defenders go in Round 1 of the 2022 NFL draft. That was a record. Such an outflow should have left substantial holes, until we note that the first player drafted – defensive end Travon Walker – was a starter only in the final of his three seasons. The Bulldogs have subs who also are great players.

Said Smart, speaking at SEC Media Days: "There's a hunger among this group. That hunger comes from the opportunity people playing behind (such lofty draftees) have to replace them."

Then: "The great news is, we've recruited well."

Georgia never was a hard sell. It's based in a state where snow isn't an annual nuisance. Its campus is

Kirby Smart speaks at SEC Media Days, held at the College Football Hall of Fame in Atlanta. (Curtis Compton/The Atlanta Journal-Constitution)

within the shadow of Atlanta. Georgia high school football is tremendous. Georgia fans are as rabid as any.

The Bulldogs, Smart reported, "have 95 players on NIL (agreements)," and such cash-on-the-barrelhead is, at least for now, A-OK. Smart again: "I don't know that what's going on is sustainable."

But what he has built is. If NIL money went away tomorrow, Georgia would still find a way to assemble the nation's deepest team. That's what Smart and his staff do. They find ways. They bring in 5-stars and coach them up, even though some assistants leave to become head coaches elsewhere.

Said Smart, who's not a braggart: "We know we're going to have a good defense year-in and year-out."

Back to that final 8:09 against Alabama: That was a case of very good players making huge plays, but also it was an indication that, in terms of aggregate talent, Smart's team had outgrown his mentor's.

"Credibility to me is earned," Smart said, and the ultimate stamp of credibility is to run down mighty Bama at the end.

He and his players, Smart said, have been talking about "how the mighty have fallen." Alabama has repeated as titlist only once under Saban. Examples of hugely gifted teams that couldn't go back-to-back include Bama in 2010, Florida State in 2014, Ohio State in 2015, Clemson in Trevor Lawrence's sophomore season.

Smart: "We didn't build this program on one-hit wonders. We built it to sustain."

And: "We will not be hunted at the University of Georgia."

This isn't to say the Bulldogs are incapable of stumbling. Any team can have a bad day. Georgia under Smart doesn't have many, though. It has been among the nation's best teams for five years. It could be the nation's best team over the next five. ∎

Kirby Smart addressed the Bulldogs' recruiting acumen and hunger for victory ahead of the 2022 season. (Curtis Compton/The Atlanta Journal-Constitution)

GEORGIA 49, OREGON 3

September 3, 2022 • Atlanta, Georgia

EVEN BETTER THAN LAST YEAR?

Reigning Champs Trounce No. 11 Ducks in Season Opener

By Mark Bradley

What Georgia did last season? What if that was but a preview? What if the really good stuff is arriving .... oh, about now? Final score (not a misprint): Georgia 49, Oregon 3.

The reigning national champ faced the Associated Press' 11th-ranked team in its season opener. If Oregon is indeed among the West's best, Georgia's third-stringers should apply for Pac-12 membership. I hear there are vacancies.

I also hear the College Football Playoff is expanding to 12. The Bulldogs have enough talent to staff two qualifiers, maybe three. Some worried about all those stalwarts lost to the NFL.

Nobody should ever fret about Georgia being caught short. Last season's team might have been the Red & Black's greatest. Come December, we might be watching a better one.

Oregon's first four possessions: punt; interception (fabulous coverage/catch by Malaki Starks); interception (Christopher Smith jumped the route); field goal after being positioned at the Georgia 11 by a personal foul.

Georgia's first four possessions: an 85-yard drive to a touchdown; a 92-yard drive to a touchdown; a 56-yard drive to a touchdown; a 75-yard drive to ... well, you know.

Stetson Bennett completed 12 of his first 14 passes – the misses were throwaways – for 181 yards. He finished the half 18-for-21, making like Fran Tarkenton to buy time and deliver to Ladd McConkey for the touchdown that made the score 28-3 at the half.

Said Kirby Smart, Georgia's coach: "We can execute at a high level. We've got an experienced quarterback."

Brock Bowers caught two passes for 38 yards and enabled McConkey's touchdown reverse by blocking a defender deep into the end zone. Darnell Washington, the 6-foot-7 tight end, hurdled a Duck – pulled a Knowshon, in UGA parlance – on a 25-yard gain. Georgia gained 314 yards in 30 minutes. If it wasn't a perfect half, it was darn close.

Flash back to the 2021 opener against Clemson in Charlotte. Georgia won 10-3.

With JT Daniels at quarterback, the Bulldogs didn't score an offensive touchdown. Granted, Clemson plays better defense than Oregon. But Georgia should play better offense in 2022 than it did last year, possibly any year.

Say what you will about Bennett – by now, haven't we said it all? – but offensive coordinator Todd Monken trusts him. To manage the game, yes, but also to control it.

Bennett distributes the ball. He can handle a fast tempo. He runs when there's nobody open. As Smart said, "He's hard to get on the ground."

Monken's offense this day resembled nothing

Georgia defensive back Malaki Starks intercepts a pass on Oregon's second drive in the first quarter. The Bulldogs' staunch defense held the No. 11 Ducks to just one field goal in the season opener. (Jason Getz/The Atlanta Journal-Constitution)

that we've seen from Georgia. In the first half, it ran 12 times for 59 yards against 21 passes for 254. In not quite three quarters, Bennett completed 25 of 31 passes for 386 yards and two touchdowns. Kenny McIntosh caught nine passes for 117 yards. That's a running back with wide receiver numbers.

The Bulldogs spread the field and left Oregon grasping. Their longest gain came on a pass to McIntosh. They were 9-for-their-first-9 on third-down conversions.

The second half commenced. Georgia took the ball at its 36. It needed six plays – four passes, then two runs by Kendall Milton, the second a delay that popped on third-and-3 – for another score.

The Bulldogs had gained 377 yards in 32 minutes and 43 seconds. They'd been favored by 16.5 points. They led 35-3, almost twice the spread in a tad more than half the game.

They weren't done scoring. Caveat: It's one game. Oregon might not be very good. (Dan Lanning's first game as head Duck won't prompt Nike to issue a commemorative shoe.) But Georgia managed 256 yards over 60 minutes in its opener on a neutral field last season; it amassed 533 yards in the first 45 minutes against Oregon, 571 in all.

Said Bennett: "Who's to say we don't run it 40 times next week? However we need to play the game to win is how we play the game."

We've been told – warned, actually – that this isn't last season's Georgia. We and Oregon just learned that there's more to this program than Jordan Davis and Nakobe Dean and Travon Walker and Zamir White and James Cook.

Smart again: "We hunt. We embrace expectations."

There's a reason Smart recruits like a maniac every year. There's always another team, another season. This Georgia team, this Georgia season, won't necessarily be worse than the last one. ■

Offensive lineman Devin Willock plows the road for running back Kenny McIntosh in the third quarter. Georgia totaled 133 yards on the ground against Oregon. (Curtis Compton/The Atlanta Journal-Constitution)

GEORGIA 33, SAMFORD 0

September 10, 2022 • Athens, Georgia

GOOD ENOUGH

Georgia Gets the Job Done Against Samford

By Chip Towers

Hey, what did you expect, Georgia to score touchdowns on every possession all season? Quarterback Stetson Bennett's streak of perfect offense ended on the Bulldogs' first drive of the game against Samford. They were stopped for no gain on third-and-3 at the Samford 5, were flagged for delay of game while contemplating going for it on fourth down and finally settled for a 27-yard field goal by Jack Podlesny.

The Bulldogs would suffer a similar fate on their second possession, too, settling for a 25-yard "J-Pod" kick. And so it went.

It was that kind of day for the defending national champions. Playing at home for the first time since November, Georgia won in spectacularly unspectacular fashion 33-0.

"I mean, there was good and there was bad," Bennett said. "There was more bad than there was last week, which is a credit to Samford. We can't take for granted who coach (Chris) Hatcher and that team is. They've got 22 seniors on their two-deep (depth chart); that's going to be a good team. But, at the end of the day, we didn't execute."

To say that the Bulldogs simply went through the motions against their FCS visitors probably would be too harsh, but not a stretch. On a damp, overcast day in Athens, there certainly wasn't the energy that was crackling throughout Mercedes-Benz Stadium a week earlier against No. 11 Oregon as Georgia turned in a near-perfect performance in a 49-3 win.

Georgia built a 30-0 halftime lead on three field goals and three touchdowns and really no highlight-reel plays. And when Bennett took a 17-yard sack in the third quarter, leading to a missed 54-yard field goal, Georgia had only its second empty offensive possession of the season.

"We didn't score touchdowns," Georgia coach Kirby Smart said. "Offensively, our goal coming into the season was, 'How can we score more touchdowns.' We come off a week where every opportunity to score a touchdown, we score a touchdown. And then we take a huge step back and have to kick field goals. Good teams can't do that."

Nevertheless, Bennett's day again ended early. He finished 24-of-34 passing for 300 yards and one touchdown. He added a rushing TD.

Carson Beck took over at quarterback at the 2:34 mark of the third quarter, and it was more of the same. His first series ended in a 25-yard field goal. That was the fourth of the day for Podlesny.

Georgia's defense did distinguish itself, however. It gave up zero points, one first down and only 59 yards on 23 plays in the opening half. Samford, which if nothing else seemingly always moves the ball against anybody with Chris Hatcher's "Hatch Attack" offense, was shut out, the ninth time for Georgia in the Smart era. The Bulldogs, as the visitors also are called, managed just 128 total yards.

Georgia posted its third takeaway of the season on a Dan Jackson hit and Xavian Sorey fumble recovery

Wide receiver Dillon Bell picks up yardage during the third quarter. Bell had three catches against Stamford, including a second-quarter touchdown to give Georgia a 20-0 lead. (Curtis Compton/The Atlanta Journal-Constitution)

in the first quarter. Freshmen cornerback Malaki Starks and defensive end Mykel Williams each started, and Williams recorded the Bulldogs' first quarterback sack of the season with a nine-yard drop in the fourth quarter.

"You win championships with defense, and they are really talented over there," Hatcher observed. "They are always in the right place, and they do such a good job of mixing their blitzes and stunts to keep you off-balance and not knowing where they're coming from. They do a great job."

The rest of the game was a blur of meaningless possessions and wholesale substitutions. By head coaches' agreement, the fourth-quarter was shortened from 15 to 12 minutes. Smart said the reason why was between him and Hatcher, who gave him his first job

in college coaching at Valdosta State. Hatcher insisted it was because of the threat of inclement weather.

There certainly was no complaining from the host team. The Bulldogs dressed 100 players and played 82 of them. In the grand scheme of a long season, the lack of stress and strain can be beneficial. But it also can be detrimental.

"How are we going to respond when it gets tough?" Smart asked rhetorically. "How are we going to play when it gets thick, gets physical, gets fast, when you're tired and give up a touchdown?" ∎

GEORGIA 48, SOUTH CAROLINA 7
September 17, 2022 • Columbia, South Carolina

A BLOWOUT

Bennett Heaves, Leads Dawgs to Dominant Win
By Chip Towers

Well, Georgia's Stetson Bennett got his Heisman Trophy moment.

The Bulldogs' star quarterback threw up right before throwing a perfectly placed 6-yard touchdown pass to Brock Bowers in the second quarter. Then he threw up again.

Yet, the sixth-year senior never left the game. Well, at least not until coach Kirby Smart finally sat him with the Bulldogs leading 38-0 midway through the third quarter.

At that point, Bennett had passed for 284 yards, thrown for two touchdowns and run for another. His was only one part of the most thoroughly dominating Georgia win over South Carolina in the 128-year history of the rivalry. Final score: 48-7.

But the critical moment, if there was one, was when Bennett threw up in the middle of the Bulldogs' 67-yard scoring drive early in the second quarter. Turns out, that wouldn't be the last time. Two plays after throwing up the first time, Bennett threw a high-arcing pass to Bowers on the left boundary of the South Carolina end zone.

Then he turned away and puked again.

"My insides just got so hot," Bennett said. "I don't know what it was. I just got hot, and it all came out of me. It happened two plays earlier, then I threw the touchdown and just immediately threw up again."

Bennett's teammates loved it. Bowers, the sophomore tight end, caught five passes for 121 yards and scored three touchdowns, including a 78-yard catch and 5-yard run. But he had no idea what Bennett was dealing with before and after he hit Bowers on the fade pattern.

"I said 'good throw' and he just said 'yeah' and seemed a little down. Then somebody told me he threw up," Bowers said. "It's awesome."

In case there was any doubt about Bennett's health, he and Bowers hooked up again on Georgia's first possession of the second half. Bowers broke open in the middle of the field and hauled in Bennett's play-action pass for a 78-yard touchdown.

Those were only two highlight plays in a day of a bunch of them. Georgia's first SEC victory of the season resulted in the largest margin ever over South Carolina. The previous mark was 40 points from Georgia's 40-0 win in 1894.

Bennett's final numbers told a story of thorough domination: 16-of-23 passing for 284 yards and two touchdowns, plus a rushing score. Bennett left the game as the Bulldogs' leading rusher with 36 yards. He would've had two more yards and another rushing TD had his foot not caught the sideline chalk on what ended up being a 15-yard run.

Yeah, this was Bennett's day. And Bowers', too.

Defensive lineman Mykel Williams celebrates after tackling South Carolina quarterback Spencer Rattler. The Bulldogs limited the Gamecocks to just one late touchdown and 306 yards of total offense. (Curtis Compton/The Atlanta Journal-Constitution)

Georgia's breakout star and leading receiver in last season's run to the national championship, Bowers scored three times on two receptions and a 5-yard run on a tight-end reverse in the first quarter. Bowers finished with five catches for 121 yards after coming into the game with five for 95 for the season.

Ten Georgia players caught passes in the game. That included freshman tight end Oscar Delp, who scored the first touchdown of his career on a 28-yard reception from quarterback Carson Beck.

All the offensive fireworks rendered another suffocating performance by Georgia's defense as a mere footnote. Freshman safety Malaki Starks grabbed his second interception of his young career and returned this one 42 yards to set up the Bulldogs' second scoring drive. Junior defensive back Dan Jackson and junior linebacker Trezmen Marshall also had picks.

Freshman defensive end Mykel Williams recorded his second sack of the season, and linebacker Jamon "Pop" Dumas-Johnson collected a team-best six tackles.

The Bulldogs kept South Carolina quarterback Spencer Rattler under duress for the duration. Rattler, the high-profile transfer from Oklahoma, was 13-of-25 passing for 118 yards and no touchdowns when Georgia's front-line defenders all headed to the sideline at the end of the third quarter.

The Gamecocks' only touchdown came with 53 seconds left in the game against Georgia's defensive backups. That was the first touchdown the Bulldogs have allowed all season. ■

Malaki Starks intercepts a pass in the first quarter, leading to Georgia's second touchdown drive. (Curtis Compton/The Atlanta Journal-Constitution)

GEORGIA 39, KENT STATE 22
September 24, 2022 • Athens, Georgia

A GROUSING VICTORY

Bulldogs Flex Composure Muscle Against Golden Flashes

By Chip Towers

Georgia probably was due for a stinker. And "stinker" might be too disrespectful a word for the Kent State Golden Flashes, who played the Bulldogs better than any team has this season after playing two of their first three games on the road against Power 5 powerhouses.

Nevertheless, Georgia fans could be heard grousing as they left Sanford Stadium and on social media throughout the game as the Bulldogs struggled at times against an opponent over which they were favored by 45.5 points.

Georgia won 39-22, but coach Kirby Smart won't have to worry this week about everybody fawning all over his team as it prepares to return to SEC play next week at Missouri. But Smart said he does know now that the Bulldogs have "a composure muscle." Coming into the game, he wasn't sure if they did while winning the previous three contests 130-10.

"It hadn't happened this year. It happened several times today," Smart said during his postgame press conference. "I thought the kids got to flex that muscle. You don't build a muscle without using it, right? We certainly got to use it today. I probably need to work on mine for sure."

Smart found himself losing his composure several times during the game. Entering the game without committing a turnover all season, the Bulldogs had three in the first half alone.

For the second week in a row, they gave up a first down on a fake punt, which Smart counts as a turnover. Leading only 32-22 well into the fourth quarter, the Bulldogs had to play their primary offensive and defensive units for the entire game. Quarterback Stetson Bennett actually finished a game on the field for the first time this season.

Kent State had Georgia's defensive starters on their heels the entire second half, with scoring drives of 10 and 11 plays, respectively. Bennett and the Bulldogs' first-string offense not only were throwing the ball in the fourth quarter, but had to. It took a 13-play touchdown drive of its own for Georgia to fully secure victory. And, then, Kendall Milton's 1-yard run didn't come until only 5:30 remained in the game.

With a 13-point final margin, Georgia tight end Brock Bowers truly was the difference in the two teams. He had two more rushing TDs - the latest covering 75 and 2 yards - to make him 3-for-3 this season on scoring when the Bulldogs hand him the football.

"I think this game was really good for us," said sophomore Bowers, who also had four catches for 54 yards. "I mean, they're a good team. They were executing and just making plays everywhere. So, I mean, they're a good team, and I'm kind of glad we had to pull it out in the fourth quarter."

Georgia finished with 529 yards, never punted and possessed the ball for 37 minutes. Kent State had only three first downs at halftime but recorded nine and 153 yards on two scoring drives totaling 25 plays spanning the third quarter and fourth quarters. ■

Wide receiver Ladd McConkey runs for extra yardage after making a catch in the third quarter. McConkey led Georgia receivers with six catches for 65 yards against Kent State. (Jason Getz/The Atlanta Journal-Constitution)

GEORGIA 26, MISSOURI 22

October 1, 2022 • Columbia, Missouri

A CLOSE CALL

Dawgs Need Fourth-Quarter Comeback to Tame Tigers

By Steve Hummer

The first Saturday in October in mid-America was a time and place to readjust the prism through which 2022 Georgia football is viewed. Maybe this season is not meant to be a three-month cakewalk to the SEC Championship game. Maybe the defending champions are not going to plow through a schedule that in places looked as soft as new-fallen snow.

There just might be more instances like the road game against Missouri when it's time to put on your Wellies and slog through the mud and be grateful for any kind of win, no matter how unsightly.

For much of the game, the Bulldogs weren't that good. But trailing a 28-point underdog by 10 points with a little more than 14 minutes to play, they screwed up the resolve to impose their will on Missouri and to take control of a contest that so often comes down to the most basic task of moving someone who doesn't want to be moved.

Bottled up for three quarters, Georgia mounted consecutive fourth-quarter touchdown drives and was able to run out the final 3:39 with one good, old-fashioned handoff after another, finishing a skinny 26-22 victory. It was a far more desperate scene than anyone could have imagined earlier this week, but the experience had certain positive qualities, too.

Coach Kirby Smart looked at a bunch that trailed 16-6 at the half, one that was being outplayed pillar to post, and determined, "It was the most together I've ever seen our team."

Quarterback Stetson Bennett had as unimpressive a 300-yard passing performance (24-of-44, 312 yards) as was possible. You can say he's in a bit of a slump. Yet he was already busy turning the evening into chicken salad just moments after leaving the field. "I think we're going to grow from it. I don't know that we need it (a close test of resolve) or any of that stuff. That's what we got, that's what we have to deal with."

Georgia was not supposed to cling to this one by a shoestring, yet the Bulldogs were not too proud to do so when called upon. See safety Malaki Starks running down breakaway Missouri back Cody Schrader, 63 yards downfield from where he started, denying him the last yard to the end zone on effort alone.

From there, Georgia was able to keep the Tigers from a touchdown, limiting them to a field goal late in the first half. Simple math: The four-point difference was kind of large.

The best part of a difficult evening was Georgia rediscovering its essential self when it was most needed.

Tight end Brock Bowers runs for a first down in the fourth quarter. Georgia ran for in a touchdown on the next play to take a 26-22 lead in the Bulldogs' closest game of the 2022 regular season. (Jason Getz/The Atlanta Journal-Constitution)

Linebacker Nolan Smith sacks Missouri quarterback Brady Cook in the second half. The Bulldogs sacked Cook twice in the win. (Jason Getz/The Atlanta Journal-Constitution)

Look, we all know by now that Georgia is no longer the sacred keeper of the run game. These days, it's no more Running Back U than it is Easy to Get Into U.

But with no running game, at least the absolute lack of one the Bulldogs trotted out for the first three quarters, that's also how you turn into Field Goal U. And Jack Podlesny, bless his steely heart and his four clutch field goals this day, is not going to kick you to a second national title.

No matter all the Bulldogs reliance upon its old-soul quarterback and its Swiss Army tight end, it just had to find a better running attack than what was being tossed out against these Tigers (61 yards rushing in the first three quarters).

"About the only time we could run it was when we had to," Smart said. His team churned out 107 fourth-quarter rushing yards, the last 43 of which came when the Bulldogs ran out the final 3:38 of the clock on eight straight carries.

"It's all a mindset," tight end Brock Bowers said. "We knew we were going to run it, they knew we were going to run it and we just had to pound them and do it better than they did."

Said football philosopher and center Sedrick Van Pran: "When you have to have it, you have to have it. Nothing else matters."

How brutal was the beginning of this one? Once, 38 years ago, after witnessing his Bulldogs lose to Georgia Tech, the famed AJC columnist Lewis Grizzard could only bring himself to write a single sentence: "Frankly, I don't want to talk about it." Then nothing but blank white space appeared beneath.

Running back Daijun Edwards scores the go-ahead 1-yard touchdown in the fourth quarter with help from offensive linemen Sedrick Van Pran and Tate Ratledge. (Jason Getz/The Atlanta Journal-Constitution)

It was that kind of brutal.

There was an almost unspeakable quality particularly to the offensive performance by the presumptive No. 1 team in the country. The Bulldogs began the evening thusly with their first four possessions:

- **Three-and-out.**
- **A lost fumble by Kendall Milton.**
- **Three-and-out after a Ladd McConkey drop.**
- **Four-and-out.**

By the first quarter, Georgia had deployed punter Brett Thorson three times, half as many as in the first four games combined. As opening statements go, it was the football equivalent of the world's worst pick-up line, akin to, "Is it hot in here, or is it just you?"

It got only marginally better in the second quarter, where during one particularly forgettable two-play sequence, Bennett had a pass attempt squirt from his hand like it was a greased honeydew melon, and then fumbled away a fake handoff in the clumsiest way.

For all that, the Bulldogs awoke when needed and stayed just as unbeaten as the world expects them to be.

The truth of this team remains complicated. The prism through which it is now viewed provides as much uncertainty as clarity. This championship business is supposed to be hard. ∎

GEORGIA 42, AUBURN 10

October 8, 2022 • Athens, Georgia

'ENJOY IT!'

Potent Rushing Attack Leads Dawgs Past SEC West Foe

By Michael Cunningham

Stetson Bennett said the expectations for Georgia's offense got out of hand after Week 1. It seemed all the offseason questions were answered once the Bulldogs hung 49 points on Oregon in the opener. They would be explosive on offense again. No more concerns about a lack of playmakers. No worries about Bennett still being The Man at quarterback.

Then the Bulldogs sputtered to 26 points in a close win at Missouri and everyone wondered what's wrong. Bennett suspects there will be similar handwringing after Georgia's offense didn't get going for nearly three quarters against Auburn. Bennett wants the Bulldogs to stop listening to that kind of talk.

"I think we do let people tell us how we should feel about a 42-10 SEC victory against Auburn," he said. "Like, enjoy it! We've got things to clean up, but that's football. We're not going to be perfect.

"We should want to be, but I don't think we should kill ourselves if we aren't."

There will come a time when the Bulldogs need to be closer to perfect to win. That wasn't necessary against Auburn. The Bulldogs are that much better than their rivals from the SEC West. Make it six consecutive victories for Georgia over Auburn, including four by a margin of 21 points or more.

Georgia's defense never yielded. Passing wasn't working early, so the Bulldogs kept pressing their advantage along the line of scrimmage. Then everything worked in the fourth quarter, when the Bulldogs scored on three consecutive possessions to put Auburn away.

"I think we are getting too (much) like, 'Argh, well, it wasn't perfect' and so then (we're) miserable," he said. "No! We played a good game. We've got a lot of things to get better at, but that's all it is. We're going to enjoy this one."

There was a lot to like for the Bulldogs. Topping the list is the way they bullied Auburn into submission by running the ball. Georgia totaled 292 yards rushing (excluding one sack) and six touchdowns, the most since 2018 vs. UMass. Four Bulldogs had rushing TDs, led by Daijun Edwards' three scores.

The way the Bulldogs finished more than made up for the way they started. They scored two touchdowns in the first half, but punted four times and missed a field-goal try. Bennett said the Bulldogs were pressing because they wanted to make amends after struggling to score at Missouri.

The Bulldogs got on track once Bennett found his rhythm. He was 7-for-13 for 25 yards before halftime. Bennett missed Brock Bowers twice and Ladd McConkey once when they were open deep. After halftime, Bennett was 15-for-19 for 183 yards and ran 64 yards for a TD to begin the fourth quarter.

The Tigers were focused on not letting Bennett

Quarterback Stetson Bennett celebrates with teammates after his 64-yard touchdown run in the fourth quarter. (Hyosub Shin/The Atlanta Journal-Constitution)

beat them with deep passes early. They stuck close to Bennett's targets on short throws and rallied to tackle pass catchers. The plan didn't work because the Tigers wore down trying to stop Georgia from running. Auburn coach Bryan Harsin didn't help matters with an ill-advised fake punt call near the end of the first quarter.

The Tigers had a fourth-and-6 at their 34-yard line in a scoreless game. Georgia's first three drives had ended with two punts and a missed field goal. Auburn lined up to punt and the snap went to John Samuel Shenker in the backfield. He tried to run to his left, but Georgia's Nolan Smith tossed aside a blocker and tackled Shenker after a two-yard gain.

The Bulldogs had a first down 36 yards away from the end zone. They needed seven plays to get there. Six of those plays were runs. First Kendall Milton, then Edwards ran through the space created by strong blocking. Auburn went three-and-out on its next possession, then McConkey returned the punt 38 yards to Auburn's 31-yard line.

Three consecutive Georgia runs produced another touchdown for a 14-0 lead. It was clear by then that the Bulldogs didn't need to score more points to win this game. Everything was hard for Auburn's offense, which couldn't produce much more than scrambles by slippery quarterback Robby Ashford.

The Bulldogs corralled Tank Bigsby, Auburn's All-SEC running back. Passing was just as hard for the Tigers. Ashford could barely get into his pass drop backs before the Bulldogs chased him out of the pocket. He couldn't find yards going side-to-side, but made some big gains when he cut back through the middle.

In the end, it was a blowout victory for the Bulldogs over one of their rivals. Bennett wanted them to feel good about that instead of fretting about the things they did wrong.

"They've got a good football team, and we beat them pretty good," Bennett said. "I think we should be happy and just keep getting better." ∎

Running back Daijun Edwards rushes for 28 yards in the first quarter. Georgia rushed for 292 yards on 39 carries against Auburn. (Curtis Compton/The Atlanta Journal-Constitution)

HEAD COACH

KIRBY SMART

Elite Coaches Juggle Football, Family and Health Amid 'The Grind'

By Chip Towers • October 14, 2022

It's called "the grind."

There's not a succinct definition. Simply put, it's the relentless schedule that consumes college football coaches during the season.

Coaches spend pretty much every Friday night on the road recruiting. Postgame Saturdays and Sunday mornings are reserved for hosting recruiting prospects and their families. Monday through Thursday is spent in acute preparation for coming opponents.

Coaches try to sneak in some quality time with their families along the way. Georgia coach Kirby Smart builds that into the weekly schedule every Thursday. But kids' football games, gymnastics meets and dance recitals can be difficult, if not impossible, to attend this time of year.

Nobody's worried about overworked college coaches these days because they are tremendously well-compensated, if not overly so. But there remain only so many days in a year and so many years in a lifetime.

Now 46 years old and Georgia's coach for the past seven seasons, Smart was asked what he does to take care of himself. He laughed.

"I should exercise more; I don't," Smart said. "I like to eat, and that doesn't couple well with not exercising. But I spend time with our players and what little time I have left I spend with my family."

Smart's health and well-being is no joking matter. The schedule, pace and never-ending stress of the "grind" are a real issue in college coaching, especially at the highest levels.

Former Georgia coach Mark Richt believes the grind contributed significantly to him developing Parkinson's disease, a diagnosis he revealed in July 2021.

"I don't think there's any doubt that it contributed to my situation," said Richt, who is a part-time college football analyst for ACC Network. "Lack of sleep especially. The only time your brain detoxes is during REM sleep. You don't get much of that as a coach. And you only get rid of the toxins in your body through exercise. So, inflammation and stress are pretty prevalent."

Parkinson's is a long-term degenerative disorder of the central nervous system. The actual cause is unknown,

Kirby Smart celebrates with fans in Atlanta after Georgia's win over LSU in the SEC Championship game. (Bob Andres/ The Atlanta Journal-Constitution)

but medical studies have determined that both inherited and environmental factors seem to play a role.

Richt coached for 35 years before retiring in 2018. He said he would routinely gain 30 to 40 pounds during the season, then try to lose it all during the offseason. Typically, he would develop a decent exercise regimen over the summer and carry it into preseason camp.

"By the end of Game 1, you feel like you don't have time to do it anymore, and you start eating whatever's there, and you don't sleep," Richt said. "The biggest triggers for Parkinson's are inflammation, toxins in your body and stress."

Smart and his wife, Mary Beth, have three children. Twins Weston and Julia turned 14 in February. Andrew turned 10 in late May. Andrew, who many of the players call "Drew," is an almost constant companion of his father at the Butts-Mehre football complex.

Amid all their other duties, coaches spend time being surrogate parents to the Bulldogs' players. The recruiting footprint of the defending national champions has increased significantly since the program's first appearance in the College Football Playoff in 2017. Including 85 players and more than two dozen walk-ons, players have signed with Georgia from as far west as California and as far south as Australia.

Part of Smart's pitch to prospects and their parents is that they can reach out to him about anything at any time.

"I can cold-call – that is the term I like to use – Kirby right now without texting him first. Him or Mary Beth, either one," said Tralee Hale, the mother of Georgia cornerback Kelee Ringo, who signed with the Bulldogs out of Phoenix. "Both of them are extremely open and flexible and accommodating. It's just unreal to imagine how Kirby juggles it all with so much going on, but he handles it."

In recruiting, Smart promises prospects that he will "coach them hard." The intention, he said, is to get the most out of their athletic potential while hopefully earning them a shot at a professional football career. But winning – right now – remains the primary objective.

"So, I love coach Smart, first off; let me get that out of the way – love him," said Xavier Truss, a fourth-year junior guard from Rhode Island. "You can text him. He's very personable with individual players. That's something I've noticed over the past four years, just how personal he can be. But, at the same time, at practice he can flip that switch and light a fire under you. He can do that, too. At the end of the day, I think that helps overall camaraderie of the team and everybody involved."

In July 2022, Smart signed a new contract that pays him an average of $11.25 million a year. For a month or so, the 10-year, $112.5 million deal made Smart the highest-paid coach in college football. Both Saban and Swinney signed new contracts in September to put them back ahead of Smart on that list.

Georgia's players know how much money all their coaches make. It's public record and routinely bantered about. They also know better than most the time and energy commitment that's involved.

"It's a lifestyle to them now, at this point in time," sophomore offensive tackle Broderick Jones said. "You know, I commend them for that. You know they have families as well, but I feel like they put in the time for their families and for us to succeed at a high level. And,

Kirby Smart celebrates with defensive back Javon Bullard after Georgia's win over Ohio State in the Peach Bowl Playoff Semifinal in Atlanta. (Jason Getz/The Atlanta Journal-Constitution)

you know, I believe their families understand that."

They do. But Matt Luke, Georgia's offensive line coach from 2019-21 and a former head coach at Ole Miss, abruptly retired in February to spend more time with his family.

And coaching tenures in general are on the decrease. A study by Business Insider in 2018 showed that the average tenure for an FBS head coach at that time was less than five years. Increased compensation along with a relentless recruiting calendar that now includes a December signing period have contributed to shorter careers.

Richt was at Miami for only four seasons after coaching at Georgia for 15.

"All year round is probably a bigger issue," he said. "You know, it's the type of job that can be a 24/7, 365-days-a-year deal. You try to carve out some down time or vacation time, but it's hard to be peaceful when there are still a lot of things on your plate that at a moment's notice need your attention, whether it's recruiting or discipline or hiring a new coach or whatever it may be."

Smart said his sanity comes in the former of regular routine.

"Sunday-Monday-Tuesday is pretty intense for our coaches," he said. "Wednesday is a little better. We go home after practice, so you get to see your family. I like to say we catch up on Wednesday. Thursday, take a deep breath and then get ready for Friday and Saturday. There's not a lot of time I have in the day to do other things."

Like diet and exercise. For now, they will have to wait. ∎

Head coach Kirby Smart stands with players before Georgia took the field against Mississippi State on November 12 in Starkville, Mississippi. (Hyosub Shin/The Atlanta Journal-Constitution)

GEORGIA 55, VANDERBILT 10

October 15, 2022 • Athens, Georgia

MISMATCH

Dominant Dawgs Dismantle Vanderbilt

By Chip Towers

Georgia's good. Vanderbilt's not.

There's not much else that needs to be known about the homecoming game conducted between the hedges at Sanford Stadium. The No. 1-ranked Bulldogs (7-0, 4-0 SEC) occasionally had to strain, but not often enough to leave any doubt about the eventual outcome, which ended in a 55-0 Georgia victory.

Notably missing several key players again because of injury, the Bulldogs punted once and took a knee once on the way to a 28-0 halftime lead. A personal-foul penalty left the Commodores with a scoring opportunity at the end of the second quarter. But then a grounding call was followed by a missed field-goal attempt.

And so it went. Even the Bulldogs' scoring drives lacked scintillating highlights. And some of the ones that were, scintillating that is, weren't.

It looked as if freshman receiver Dillon Bell had gone 66 yards for a touchdown with a catch midway through the first quarter. But an exhaustive video-replay review determined his elbow had touched the ground on the attempted tackle. Same thing happened on what appeared like a beautiful toe-tapping grab by Kearis Jackson late in the game.

No matter. The Bulldogs simply proceeded with an offensive formula they would stick with all day. That is, no-nonsense demonstrations of fundamental football executed with superior personnel.

Georgia offensive coordinator Todd Monken was nothing if not patient calling plays. Ten plays, 75 yards; four plays, 42 yards; 11 plays, 81 yards; 10 plays, 55 yards. So went the Bulldogs' offense, which was more than happy to possess the football for nearly $20\frac{1}{2}$ of the game's first 30 minutes and 39 of the full 60.

"They were playing really deep with their safeties; they got back," said Georgia quarterback Stetson Bennett, who broke a three-game streak without a passing touchdown with two in the first half. "When that happens, it's hard to hit shot plays. But it's easy to throw underneath and get first downs, get 6 (yards), get 7, get 15 and move down the field. If they make you do it, then you've gotta do it."

Accordingly, Georgia piled up 30 first downs while calling 41 pass plays and 38 rushes.

The last drive of the opening half typified the slow bleed of Vanderbilt that characterized the afternoon. There was a 34-yard pass to Darnell Washington to start the drive and a 21-yarder to Ladd McConkey on third down in the middle of it. That was the first of three third-down conversions. The last one was a 10-yard touchdown pass to Dominick Blaylock.

PAT, kickoff, defensive stop, repeat.

Washington was the star of the day, if there was one. The 6-foot-7, 280-pound tight end from Las Vegas recorded career highs with four catches and 78 yards receiving. Daijun Edwards scored his fifth TD of the season and led the Bulldogs with 49 yards on 10

Georgia backup quarterback Carson Beck attempts a pass during the fourth quarter against Vanderbilt. Beck entered the game late in the third quarter and threw two touchdown passes in Georgia's 55-0 win. (Jason Getz/The Atlanta Journal-Constitution)

carries. What was left of the crowd got pretty excited when tight end Arik Gilbert hauled in the first TD of his Georgia career on a 4-yard pass from Carson Beck.

By then, Bennett and most of the other Georgia starters were out of the game. The last play for the Bulldogs' starting quarterback was holding for a 35-yard Jack Podlesny field goal. The play before, he was lit up on a hard tackle as he ran out of bounds on the Vanderbilt sideline and came up windmilling his right shoulder.

The Commodores could do nothing on offense. Their 10th first down didn't come until the play on which the final buzzer sounded. That gave them 150 yards – total. They were 5-of-13 on third downs.

"We still feel like we missed a lot of opportunities on the ball when it was up in the air," Georgia linebacker Jamon Dumas-Johnson said. "We got a punch-out, and that's what we were looking to do. Once you get one, they start coming in bunches."

"We got to play a lot of players," Smart said. "We're a beat-up, banged-up football team going into the off-week. It's going to be important that we give these guys (time) to get well." ∎

GEORGIA 42, FLORIDA 20
October 29, 2022 • Jacksonville, Florida

A SPECIAL WIN

Georgia Honors Vince Dooley with Hard-Fought Victory Over Florida
By Chip Towers

It was a game that would've made Vince Dooley proud. Never mind the imperfection in Georgia's 42-20 victory over Florida. The victory kept the No. 1-ranked Bulldogs undefeated on the season and continued their domination of the Gators under coach Kirby Smart.

Georgia also dominated the Florida series under Dooley, who died Oct. 28 in Athens. The Bulldogs dedicated the game to the legendary Hall of Fame coach.

But Georgia didn't make its fifth win in the past six against Florida easy. After the Bulldogs carried a 25-point lead into halftime, the Gators got to within one score, 28-20, with 3:31 still remaining in the third quarter.

That's when the Bulldogs went old school, Dooley-style. They answered with a six-play, 78-yard touchdown drive that featured five runs and one pass to make the score 35-20. After getting the ball back from Florida on downs, Georgia capped another scoring drive with its fourth rushing touchdown of the night and second by Kenny McIntosh. At that point, it was clear the Gators would be vanquished again.

"I'm sure coach Dooley enjoyed that; I'm sure he was watching," Georgia quarterback Stetson Bennett said. "You know, sometimes you take what they give you and sometimes you give them what they're gonna take."

Smart told the players in the locker room they were going to dedicate their efforts to Dooley. He said he visited with Dooley a few days earlier in the UGA football training room "not knowing it was going to be the last time I talked to him." The Bulldogs found out Dooley had died upon their plane's arrival in Jacksonville the day before the game when the coaching staff's phones lit up with text messages.

"I know if he was looking down on that one he would have enjoyed the first half; I don't know if he would have enjoyed the second one," Smart cracked. "He and Erk (Russell) probably had a laugh together about it. (Dooley has) meant so much to us. In honor of him and their family, it was special."

The Bulldogs seemed to be in total control of the game when the teams adjourned to the locker room at halftime. Georgia's Ladd McConkey scored on a touchdown pass from Bennett with 17 seconds remaining in the first half to go ahead by the ominous score of 28-3.

But the first 14 minutes of the third quarter all belonged to the Gators. After logging only two first downs in the first half, they got four times that number in the third stanza alone.

Florida started the second half with a 13-play, 75-yard touchdown drive that was aided by a personal-

Quarterback Stetson Bennett reacts to Florida fans after Kenny McIntosh's 4-yard touchdown run in the fourth quarter. (Hyosub Shin/The Atlanta Journal-Constitution)

foul penalty against Georgia freshman defensive lineman Bear Alexander. He didn't hear the whistle on a fourth-down play in which Smart called a pre-snap timeout and Alexander ran into quarterback Anthony Richardson, who had stopped his drop-back.

Then Georgia caught the turnover bug. On the Bulldogs' first possession of the second half, McIntosh had the ball yanked loose from behind linebacker Amari Burney, and Florida's Trey Dean recovered at the Georgia 27. It took seven plays to go 18 yards, but the Gators got a field goal out of it.

Next Bulldogs' possession, Georgia moved quickly down the field with two McIntosh runs totaling 33 yards. But on the third play of the drive, Bennett severely underthrew running back Daijun Edwards on a wheel route. Burney dove for the interception, which also came with a personal-foul penalty against the Gators. That backed them up to their 18-yard line.

On third-and-6, receiver Xzavier Henderson ran free down the right sideline on a busted coverage by freshman safety Malaki Starks. The 78-yard touchdown was the longest play of Henderson's career and made it a one-score game, at 28-20.

The Bulldogs answered with an offensive possession that surely had Dooley high-fiving Russell in heaven. Georgia ran the ball five times on a six-play drive that ended with a 22-yard touchdown run by Daijun Edwards. It was Edwards' second touchdown run of the game and the Bulldogs' fourth of the game. At that point, Georgia had gained less than 200 yards rushing. It would finish with 239.

Edwards finished with 106 yards rushing and McIntosh with 90. The Bulldogs averaged 6 yards per carry.

"I thought Kenny showed a little something tonight now," Smart said of the senior from Fort Lauderdale. "When he came out after that fumble, he had that eye of the tiger, and he wanted the ball. He was running the ball hard and physical and getting yards after contact. That's a lot of credit to the offensive line and a lot of credit to Kenny as well. That drive was big for us."

The victory was the Bulldogs' fifth in the past six

meetings with Florida under Smart. Dooley was 17-7-1 against the Gators.

"We talked about (Dooley) before the game and said 'let's win it for him," said Georgia tight end Brock Bowers, who had a career-best 154 yards receiving and a touchdown in the game. "To honor him was just awesome."

There were many flaws exposed for Georgia, within the third quarter in particular. The Bulldogs' secondary continues to give up explosive plays on deep pass plays down the sidelines. That's not good news with No. 3-ranked Tennessee and its fleet-footed passing game coming to Athens next week. The Gators finished with 371 yards after managing only 88 in the first half and ended with 16 first downs.

Meanwhile, after getting back star defensive tackle Jalen Carter from a knee sprain that kept him out the past four weeks, the Bulldogs lost senior outside linebacker Nolan Smith to what might be a separated shoulder late in the first quarter.

All of the above goes far in explaining why linebacker Jamon Dumas-Johnson - aka "Pop" - was far from celebratory in postgame interviews.

"Nah, I'm not," Dumas-Johnson said when asked if he was happy. "I mean, as a leader on this defense, we have higher expectations. We failed to live up with them today. The bigger thing is the 'W' or 'L' and we got the 'W' today."

While Georgia's offense played well, with another 40-plus point effort and 555 yards offense, Bennett's play was spotty against the Gators defense that came in ranked last in FBS in third-down conversions. Bennett finished with 316 yards passing and two touchdowns, but threw two interceptions and completed only 50 percent of 38 passes.

McConkey had four catches for 51 yards and a TD, but had another drop. Also, tight end Darnell Washington and slotback Dominick Blaylock each saw passes that hit their hands first end up in possession of Gators.

But the highlight of the game came on Georgia's fifth offensive possession. Bennett unleashed a

Head coach Kirby Smart celebrates with Georgia players after Georgia's 42-20 win over Florida in Jacksonville. (Hyosub Shin/The Atlanta Journal-Constitution)

throw toward Bowers, who was tightly covered by Burney running stride-for-stride with him down the left sideline in front of Georgia's bench. Burney tipped the ball, but fell down in the process. Bowers eventually hauled in the pass, but only after bobbling the ball several times.

When Bowers finally gained control, there was nobody between him and the end zone. He was untouched the rest of the way for a 73-yard touchdown.

"I just saw the ball bouncing around and snatched it out of the air," Bowers said. "I was surprised I caught it, to be honest. I didn't run as good of a route as I wanted."

In many ways, though, it was the imperfections that made Georgia's victory beautiful. To overwhelm an SEC opponent while not playing your best says a lot about toughness and resiliency.

"I don't enjoy losing the momentum in a game; I enjoy the fact that we never blinked," Smart said. "The kids were saying the right things on the sideline. You know, there's two things when adversity hits: You fracture, or you connect. And our team connected."

Said sophomore center Sedrick Van Pran: "I just want to send out my condolences to the Dooley family. Coach mentioned it in the pregame meal today, and we just wanted to go out there today and glorify his name." ∎

GEORGIA 27, TENNESSEE 13

November 5, 2022 • Athens, Georgia

'BUSINESS, NOT PERSONAL'

Georgia Defense Quiets Tennessee's Hype

By Michael Cunningham

Georgia fans started the "overrated" chant at Sanford Stadium with more than eight minutes remaining in the game. I understand the sentiment, but those hecklers got it wrong. The Volunteers had a legitimate claim to the top spot in the College Football Playoff poll. It's just that not even Tennessee's video-game offense can do much against Georgia's ferocious defense.

It wasn't clear that would be the case. After the Bulldogs beat Florida, coach Kirby Smart said his defense this year isn't quite as good as last season's all-time great group. Smart attributed Florida's second-half rally to Georgia's thin defensive front wearing down. The Gators hit on a couple of long passes and missed a few other chances because of inaccurate throws.

That raised the possibility that Tennessee's No. 1 scoring offense could poke holes in Georgia's defense. That was my reasoning for predicting a close win for the Bulldogs. Instead, Georgia, favored by $9\frac{1}{2}$ points at kickoff, won 27-13. Even that two-touchdown margin was misleading.

The Bulldogs ran to a 21-3 advantage, and Tennessee never got within 15 points of the lead until it was much too late. The Vols couldn't stage a comeback because Georgia squeezed the spirit from their celebrated offense. Tennessee scored the fewest points in 21 games with Josh Heupel as coach.

It turns out there wasn't anything to the talk about the Vols finding cracks in Georgia's defense. If all that praise for Tennessee's offense bothered the Bulldogs, they weren't saying.

"Business, not personal," Georgia linebacker Smael Mondon said.

"Our team understood the plan and stuck to the plan," Smart said.

On defense, that meant pressuring quarterback Hendon Hooker without the benefit of extra pass rushers. The Bulldogs frequently lined up with only three down linemen. Tennessee plays fast, so Georgia focused on lining up faster. Georgia's defensive backs often had to cover their assignments alone.

The Bulldogs did all of that while winning the line of scrimmage and punishing ballcarriers.

"Physical toughness won out today for us because they are a really physical team," Smart said. "They are extremely physical. They run the ball between the tackles, and until you take that away, it doesn't matter what you do outside."

Georgia defenders were everywhere the Vols tried to make plays: inside and outside, short and deep. Tennessee's offense hadn't looked this inept since scoring just 17 points against Georgia in Week 10 last season. The only other time Heupel's Vols failed to score at least 24 points was in a 38-14 loss at Florida in his first SEC game as Tennessee's coach.

Heupel's offense had reached a new level of

Georgia defenders bring down Tennessee running back Jaylen Wright during the first half. The Bulldogs limited the Vols to just 94 net rushing yards and sacked Tennessee quarterback Hendon Hooker six times. (Hyosub Shin/The Atlanta Journal-Constitution)

mystique in Year 2 at Tennessee. The Bulldogs are the first team to take it down a peg. The Vols sliced through Alabama, LSU and Kentucky. Those teams are very good on defense. They were no match for Tennessee's fast pace, tough running and big pass plays.

The Vols couldn't deal with Georgia's speed and soundness or the home crowd's noise.

"Going into the game, we said we're not going to give them any layups," Smart said. "If they go in for a layup, we're fouling them."

Smart borrowed a phrase from basketball to make the point that the Bulldogs weren't going to allow anything easy to the Vols. They would have to work hard to make plays. When they did gain ground, the Bulldogs would make them pay physically.

That's how it went for Tennessee. Hooker missed on a couple of open deep shots, but otherwise, there were no opportunities for big plays until garbage time. Georgia got to Hooker for six sacks and constant pressure. Runs also weren't working for the Vols. The crowd noise made everything harder – Tennessee was penalized for seven false starts.

The only nit to pick with the Bulldogs was that their offense failed to deliver a knockout blow. Georgia totaled 21 points on five drives in the first 16 minutes and six points on five drives over the final 44 minutes. The Bulldogs lost two fumbles and failed to gain a first down with a chance to put Tennessee away late.

Normally, the Bulldogs sputtering to score like that would raise alarms about what happens when they need to score a lot of points to win. But if that didn't happen against Tennessee, will it ever?

The Vols had 54 plays of 20-plus yards in their first eight games. Star wide receiver Jalin Hyatt had 15 of those long gains. The Vols had no gains of 20 yards or more against Georgia until the final five minutes. Hyatt had five catches for 35 yards with a long of 15 up to that point, and Tennessee's backs had gained 74 yards on 23 carries.

Tennessee's troubles started with a mistake by its special teams. The Vols, trailing 7-3, forced a three-and-out. Tennessee's return man let Brett Thorson's punt bounce near the 20-yard line. The ball rolled and rolled until it went out of bounds at the 1-yard line. The Vols already were having trouble with the crowd noise. Now they were backed up at the enclosed end of the stadium.

Two Tennessee runs went nowhere. Hooker dropped back to pass on third down. Georgia's Jalen Carter hit him as he tried to throw in the end zone. Offensive linemen Javontez Spraggins scooped up the ball and tried to advance it out of the end zone. Field officials ruled he was down at the 1-yard line.

It was a bad call, but it turns out it hardly mattered. The Bulldogs scored on the first play of the next drive. Ladd McConkey juked a safety and ran free for a 37-yard touchdown pass from Stetson Bennett. Tennessee ran four plays on its next possession before punting. Georgia needed only six plays to score on its next drive. Bennett threw another TD pass, this one to Marcus Rosemy-Jacksaint for five yards.

Tennessee's next drive ended with a field goal after back-to-back false-start penalties turned a third-and-short into a third-and-long. The Bulldogs lost some energy after that. They gained just one first down on their next drive before punting. Then Hooker converted a fourth-down run at Georgia's 39-yard line.

The stadium got quieter. This was Tennessee's chance to get back in the game. Hooker tried a deep pass to Cedric Tillman down the right sideline. It was too deep: Georgia's Kelee Ringo caught Hooker's pass in the end zone. It was clear that Tennessee's much-hyped offense was no match for Georgia's defense, which may not be as good as last year's group, but is still great.

After closing out the victory, Bulldogs players didn't celebrate much on the field.

"They know humility is a week away," Smart said.

The Vols know all about that. They came to Athens with an offense that looked unstoppable and left with their heads down after the Bulldogs humbled them. ■

Ladd McConkey's 37-yard touchdown reception gave Georgia a 14-3 first-quarter lead. (Jason Getz/The Atlanta Journal-Constitution)

BUILT DAWG TOUGH

Bulldogs Reap Benefits of Intense Preparation

By Connor Riley • November 10, 2022

Want to know why Georgia has been the best program in college football for the past two seasons?

Maybe it's because it's the toughest one. Just ask the players.

"If you're on the field, you're a starter. We know you're tough enough and capable to do what you need to do," defensive back Kelee Ringo said.

Added receiver Marcus Rosemy-Jacksaint, "Not everybody is built to play here."

The Tennessee game in November illustrated the mental and physical toughness of the program for Ringo and Rosemy-Jacksaint. The hero of the national-title win over Alabama a season before, Ringo was having a tough week of practice, and coach Kirby Smart let him know about it – quite loudly.

After the game, in which Ringo had an interception during a dominant defensive performance, the coach jumped into his arms, and Ringo whispered, "Thank you for believing in me."

"We hit mentally tough and physically tough. They get that speech before they come," Smart said. "So we tell them, 'We're going to be physical. And we're going to practice physical; we're going to be physical in the spring. We're going to be comfortable being physical.' So that's agreed upon when they come."

Watching Tennessee quarterback Hendon Hooker struggle to overcome four quarters of physical pounding brought back some memories for Rosemy-Jacksaint. As a freshman, he recalls going over the middle of the field to catch a pass during practice. As he was running a deep route, he failed to see safety Richard LeCounte.

Bang. The senior safety put the young wide receiver on the ground, unofficially welcoming him to Georgia football.

"It's every single day," Rosemy-Jacksaint said. "That's something we have to embrace because that's how we play our game of football."

Preaching toughness, both mental and physical, is not reserved only for big games. It happens in the spring, it happens during summer workouts and most important, it happens during preseason camp.

"When you come to a place like UGA and the recruiting that this staff has done, you're going to have great players," senior offensive lineman Warren Ericson said. "How intense we practice and the standard we set for us each day, we're ready to play."

Preparation has led to major success on the field the past two seasons, and it's been mental and physical toughness that helped prepare Georgia to defeat all challenges during the 2022 season.

"Playing here is really tough. Everybody sees the rewards of us playing on Saturday, but no one sees what goes inside, coming in at 6 o'clock in the morning," Rosemy-Jacksaint said. "Going through spring, going through fall, going through the summer. All of it is mentally and physically exhausting. It's not built for everybody. Not everybody is built to play here. It's a tough place to play." ∎

Wide receiver Marcus Rosemy-Jacksaint leaps to pull in a touchdown pass during Georgia's November 5 win over Tennessee. (Hyosub Shin/The Atlanta Journal-Constitution)

GEORGIA 45, MISSISSIPPI STATE 19

November 12, 2022 • Starkville, Mississippi

DIVISION CHAMPS AGAIN

Early Second-Half Blitz Propels Georgia to SEC East Title

By Steve Hummer

The worst 44 seconds of a thus-far unbeaten campaign was bad for Georgia. Seriously bad. The kind of bad that makes a man question his faith and doubt the existence of a higher football power.

"Very, very poor job of managing the before-the-half situation, as bad as I've ever been a part of," Georgia's Kirby Smart said in the immediate aftermath of the game.

To be fair, Georgia defeated Mississippi State by 26 points (45-19).

In the process, these Bulldogs clinched their fifth SEC East title in six years. With big victories over momentary No. 1 Tennessee and a Mississippi State team that always is a tough piece of gristle to chew, they are turning what appeared to be the most treacherous part of their schedule into a relative three-week cruise, minus the sunburn and crippling lower GI issues.

And, oh, next week's foe, Kentucky, once feared for no empirical reason, just lost to Vanderbilt, who seemingly hadn't won in the conference since Jimmy Carter wore a onesie.

But sometimes you must recognize the bad to really get at how deeply good a team can be.

And, so, there were 44 seconds of ugliness, when bad coaching, bad execution and just a touch of hubris gave Mississippi State a spark of life.

Taking over on its 20 with less than a minute to go in the half, UGA opted not to do the safe, sane thing by running out the clock and taking a 17-6 lead into the locker room, comfortable in the knowledge it would get the second-half kickoff.

Rather, it got a little full of itself, a little drunk on its own success perhaps. Following a couple of incompletions on second-and-3 and third-and-3 (a called run that quarterback Stetson Bennett opted out of) – rather than running the ball for a first down or otherwise exhausting the clock – the nation's No. 1 team punted.

And then got exactly what it deserved.

Mississippi State's Zavion Thomas returned it 63 yards for a TD with only three seconds left, turning what had been a pretty comfortable first 30 minutes into a pair of bike shorts two sizes too small.

So, this is the point where a really good team determines that it will stop the nonsense before it becomes a rapidly spreading virus and start stepping on throats. That has become the mark of Georgia's majesty this season.

Bennett said there is no magic toggle on this team. "It's not like we're saving ourselves. We go every play like we're trying to do something. It's not like we flip a switch or something."

Yet Georgia set the beginning of the second half as

Ladd McConkey celebrates after scoring a touchdown in the third quarter. McConkey scored two touchdowns in the win over Mississippi State. (Hyosub Shin/The Atlanta Journal-Constitution)

a time to turn it on. "We thought that would define the second half, to take the crowd out of it if we could get some momentum back," Smart said. And then right on cue went about owning that moment in the way that only a superbly good team could.

In less than six minutes, Georgia turned all the doubts to dust, receiver Ladd McConkey scoring twice, once by ground, once by air. The worst 44 seconds of a season were turned to a footnote that no one will read.

The second play of the second half was a reverse toss to McConkey that went 70 yards, a perfect mixture of his speed and the devastating power of 6-foot-7 tight end Darnell Washington running downfield and seemingly downhill on a mission to part the sea of defenders.

With its second possession, Georgia moved a bit less impatiently, but still found the same end zone when Bennett found McConkey on a 17-yard touchdown pass.

Less than six minutes gone in the second half, UGA had restored order and made the thousands of fans trailing it here believe in full again.

These Bulldogs would win the second half 28-7.

Their defense would summon a couple of fourth-down stands, the most singular being when cornerback Kamari Lassiter flew like a spinning saw blade into Jo'quavious Marks, cutting him down just short of a first down at the Georgia 8 with 9:54 left in the game. And along the way neutralize the bothersome passing game of Miss State's Mike Leach, much as it had Tennessee's the week before.

They would not be rattled by the famous cowbells wielded like a weapon by Mississippi State's home crowd. Please, fool. If you're going to unsettle such a mentally well-conditioned team as this, you better bring nothing less than 40,000 tornado sirens to the game.

Sure, any cow within Oktibbeha County here may not give milk for the rest of the weekend. But as for Georgia's Bulldogs, they were nonplussed and efficiently merciless. To them, it was but the sound of crickets.

They were suckered into a false-start penalty on their first play of the game, but never again. Two plays later Georgia had its initial first down, with 19 more to come this night. Four minutes later it had its first of six touchdowns.

Sewing up the SEC East was met with all the enthusiasm of Entenmann's turning out another sweet Danish. "It's one more step to our end goal," McConkey said.

A date with LSU is set for Dec. 3 for the SEC Championship game inside Mercedes-Benz Stadium.

Enjoying every frigid moment – the good so massively outweighing the bad – was another huge following of Georgia fans.

They had made themselves known all along the road to this remote outpost, a 280-mile drive from Atlanta. The route just happens to pass right by Tuscaloosa, which to the disappointment of none, will be as close as any Bulldog gets to the University of Alabama this season. In quirky 2022, the home of the Crimson Tide is but a place to gas up and relieve oneself on the way to another special season. ■

Georgia defensive lineman Jalen Carter pressures Mississippi State quarterback Will Rogers during the third quarter. (Jason Getz/The Atlanta Journal-Constitution)

0

TIGHT END

DARNELL WASHINGTON

Georgia's 'Matchup Nightmare' Plays the Game to Its Fullest

By Mike Griffith • December 19, 2022

It didn't take long for Georgia tight end Darnell Washington to show that he would be a force to reckon with during the 2022 season.

After all, at 6-foot-7 and 285 pounds, Washington has the size and strength to dominate on the field. In the season opener against Oregon at Mercedes-Benz Stadium, Washington showed the football world that he's pretty good in the air as well.

In the air?

Yes, the physically imposing tight end hurdled a would-be tackler during a run after a catch – to the delight of teammates and fans, and the video of the leap became a viral sensation.

The player labeled as a "matchup nightmare" can run, block and now hurdle? Washington would become the ultimate weapon for the Bulldogs, and it all began with the physical traits that are hard to ignore.

"You don't find many tight ends his size," Tennessee linebackers coach Brian Jean-Mary said of Washington.

"I haven't seen anyone put together like Darnell Washington ... ever," said Cole Cubelic, a former SEC center at Auburn and current SEC Network analyst. "His upper body is in an offensive tackle frame, but then he has an inside linebacker waist, and guard quads and then he has defensive end ankles."

The big man played a big role for the Bulldogs, and it's primarily because he's made big changes after arriving in Athens before the 2020 season. A 5-star recruit from Las Vegas, Washington was in for a surprise during his first few practices in Athens.

"My first game here, my first time blocking somebody, it wasn't really pretty," Washington said. "I was like, I have to flip the switch. My 'want-to' got bigger, my 'why' got bigger, and things like that."

His growth as a player has matched his size and ability, and Georgia opponents paid the price during the season. Washington's receiving statistics are not overwhelming – especially with John Mackey Award winner Brock Bowers playing the same position – but Washington has done most of his damage without the ball in his hands.

"He blocks, he runs routes, he does everything for

Darnell Washington's unique combination of size, skill and athleticism makes it hard to find a comparable player at the tight end position. (Jason Getz/The Atlanta Journal-Constitution)

us," Georgia receiver Ladd McConkey said. "He's a huge weapon. Not just blocking, but catching the ball. You see it on those runs he has, he's so hard to tackle."

Added Tennessee's Jean-Mary: "The thing that's impressive about him is his ability to play in space, not just to block – you can throw him the ball downfield, which presents its challenges because of his size."

Another example of Washington playing big at the right time – his crushing block that paved the way for McConkey's 70-yard touchdown run against Mississippi State in a victory that ultimately clinched the SEC Eastern Division title.

"Scoring touchdowns is a fun feeling," Washington said, "but also springing one with the lead block is also a good feeling. I just live life and play the game to the fullest."

Living life and playing the game to the fullest has helped Washington earn high praise from NFL scouts – "Washington's rare blend of size and athleticism might be too much to pass up at the tight end spot," according to 19-year NFL draft scout Luke Easterling – but he's had a larger-than-life impact on almost everyone around him.

When asked to whom he would compare Washington as a player, Georgia coach Kirby Smart responded: 'The combination of athleticism and displacement, probably no one. He has a receiving skill set that's unique and, combined with that, size."

"He's a mismatch everywhere," Georgia quarterback Stetson Bennett said. "He weighs whatever he weighs, but he's like 6-8, 6-7 and can run like we run. You can't cover him with a DB. He's unbelievable." ■

Catches and touchdowns from a tight end stand out in the box score, but Darnell Washington takes pride in blocking and in the physical side of the game as well. (Jason Getz/ The Atlanta Journal-Constitution)

GEORGIA 16, KENTUCKY 6
November 19, 2022 • Lexington, Kentucky

HUMAN AFTER ALL

Dawgs Top Cats in Frigid Conditions

By Steve Hummer

Georgia is cold.

Georgia is tired.

Don't let the No. 1 ranking and the fact that it has forgotten how to lose before December fool you. Georgia, it can be reported, is human.

Anyone's going to feel frigid with a 25-mph wind blowing up his blouse. Even some indomitable Dogs.

The Bulldogs who beat Kentucky 16-6 clearly were a bunch showing all the mental and physical crow's feet that come with running the table when that table has all the barbed wire and broken glass of an SEC schedule. For the second consecutive year, they've gone unbeaten over the regular course of the conference, a feat worth pausing to appreciate even though the goal is now, and maybe forever, grander than that. Just never get the idea that such a run is easy or comes without several heavy bales of fatigue.

Georgia betrayed some worn-down-to-the-nub tendencies. It wobbled a bit. It was outplayed and out-toughed in some important fourth-quarter situations. But it won, and on a day that other top-tier teams such as TCU and Michigan barely escaped, at least this one ended with the better team taking a knee at the end. Winning always will be enough.

Kirby Smart fought the temptation to call this a lethargic win. "But it was very ho-hum," the Georgia coach allowed.

Here was a coach admitting to the grind, on a cold late November day when the other team decides to try to prove something against college football's currently preeminent program: "I feel like everybody across the league — including us — are at a point (of exhaustion), where we just had four games in a row, three on the road, that were really tough and really physical," Smart said, referring to the most current Florida-Tennessee-Mississippi State-Kentucky stretch.

"We knew this gauntlet was coming, and our guys put their heads down and worked really hard," Smart said. "Regardless of who we've faced, we stood up to the test that we've been asked to and am proud of what they've done."

Georgia also is stubborn. Smart helped keep Kentucky engaged with his decision to go for it on fourth-and-goal at the 1 to start the fourth quarter rather than kick a field goal and give the Bulldogs a three-score, 19-0 lead. "I made that decision 15 years ago," Smart said, referring to his native aggressive philosophy. Most times, that is a wonderful trait. But when Georgia was repelled this time, it gave the Wildcats a second wind. Sometimes simple math should outweigh bravado.

The same Bulldogs defense that made its own big fourth-down stand in the first half, along with a drive-killing end-zone interception, then gave up a 99-yard

Stetson Bennett wasn't at his best in the win against Kentucky, throwing for just 116 yards and an interception. (Jason Getz/The Atlanta Journal-Constitution)

touchdown drive to Kentucky. And with nearly 10 minutes left, some unnecessary suspense sneaked onto the field.

This is not a defense that gives up length-of-the-field drives. Not if its tank is anywhere near full.

"I thought we were swarming to the ball real well in the first half," noted linebacker Smael Mondon.

Come a fourth quarter in which Georgia was outgained 171-47 and outscored 6-0, in which the Bulldogs didn't attempt a single pass while Kentucky's Will Levis was throwing all over the lot, it became a matter of survival.

After giving up the long drive, Mondon said it was up to his guys to, "just stay composed, and then the next time we have a chance, go out there and put our best foot forward."

The struggle of this day was quite evident behind center. Over this remarkable calendar year, dating to the College Football Playoff Championship game, Georgia quarterback Stetson Bennett and his defense have toppled the likes of Alabama's Bryce Young, Oregon's Bo Nix, Florida's Anthony Richardson and Tennessee's Hendon Hooker. All these, plus Levis, either on performance or potential, are alleged to have more of the NFL quarterbacking essentials than Bennett.

Bennett's modest physical build always is an issue lurking in the background. Maybe just a little more prominent here in horse country, where they judge so many of the local athletes by physical conformation.

From toe to head, Bennett stands not quite 18 hands high, grand by thoroughbred measurement, but below average for a quarterback needing to see over onrushing brutes. His opponent Saturday had a good four inches on him, a usual disadvantage.

Nothing in the bloodlines suggested championship stuff for this famously redshirted QB. Bennett's saga is built upon the sediment of

disinterested recruiters and a season spent throwing the rock for Jones College in Somewhere, Miss. He is the Seabiscuit of college quarterbacks.

In all cases, helped immensely by the fact that he doesn't have to face his own dastardly defense, Bennett has had the last laugh on that roster of higher-rated quarterbacks.

But don't ever think his story is so charmed that this comes easily. In getting past Levis, too, Bennett admitted he gets cold and weary as well. He had trouble warming up before kickoff, he said, fighting the gusty wind and throwing some plug ugly balls. The result: an early overthrow of a wide open Darnell Washington and a bad interception in which Bennett said he misread a safety.

And in the end, he had to be content going back to his old game-management mode, throwing for a mere 116 yards while putting it in a running back's belly 46 times.

Is Bennett happy handing it off almost exclusively at the end?

"If we have to and we come out of here with a win, yes," he said. "I knew it was going to be tough. I don't care how often we run it."

When you're tired and you're cold, you just want to warm your hands on a win in any form.

You're only human after all. ∎

Broderick Jones helped pave the way for a Georgia rushing attack that ran for 247 yards, highlighted by 19 carries for 143 yards and a touchdown by Kenny McIntosh. (Jason Getz/The Atlanta Journal-Constitution)

LEGACY AND LEGEND

Former Players, Other Notables Attend Celebration of Vince Dooley

By Doug Roberson • November 25, 2022

Billy Payne shared a story about Vince Dooley during a celebration of the former University of Georgia coach and athletic director's life.

In the fall of 1964, Dooley showed up to recruit Payne at one of his Dykes High School football games. Payne knew Dooley would be there. He was nervous. After the game, Dooley walked up to Payne and reached out his right hand. As the two shook hands, Dooley reached around Payne with his left hand and gave him a hug.

Fifty-eight years after that hug, the two shared what would be a final hug as they sat on a couch in Dooley's home in Athens. It was the day before Dooley died. The two spoke about many things, but the first was Dooley asking if Payne remembered dropping a critical pass against Auburn in 1966. He was a coach until the end. But Payne, and the nine other speakers during a celebration of Dooley's life held at Stegeman Coliseum, said he was so much more.

"He was a teacher, not just of football skills, but of life skills," Payne said. "He taught us the importance of integrity by demonstrating the skill every single day of his life."

The ceremony was supposed to last an hour. It lasted almost two because the anecdotes were many, the reverence deep. Among those who spoke were Gov. Brian Kemp, football coach Kirby Smart, Georgia president Jere Morehead, athletic director Josh Brooks, SEC Commissioner Greg Sankey, former swimming and diving coach Jack Bauerle, former players Willie McClendon and Frank Ros and senior associate athletic director Glada Horvat.

The university held the upbeat memorial ahead of the Nov. 26 football game against Georgia Tech, which will be played at Dooley Field at Sanford Stadium.

The floor of Stegeman was divided into two sections with 12 rows in each. On the left were Dooley's family, friends and their guests. There were at least 100 people. On the right were his former players. There were at least 120 people there too.

In the stands of Stegeman were a few hundred more people, mostly dressed in red and black who came to appreciate Dooley.

Each speaker tried to highlight an aspect of Dooley that made him successful as a coach, athletic director, author or gardener, among the many things he enjoyed.

Smart shared how he was in the dining hall recently and there sat Dooley, just observing the athletes. Dooley was struggling to talk, but Smart said that even then he made him feel like the most important person on Earth.

Smart, a father, also knows the sacrifices Dooley made with regard to his family as he struggled to turn Georgia into one of the elites in college sports.

"I know the sacrifices he made to put Georgia on the map," Smart said. "He paved the way with a

Vince Dooley waves to fans during his 90th birthday honors ahead of Georgia's game against Oregon on September 3, 2022. (Jason Getz/The Atlanta Journal-Constitution)

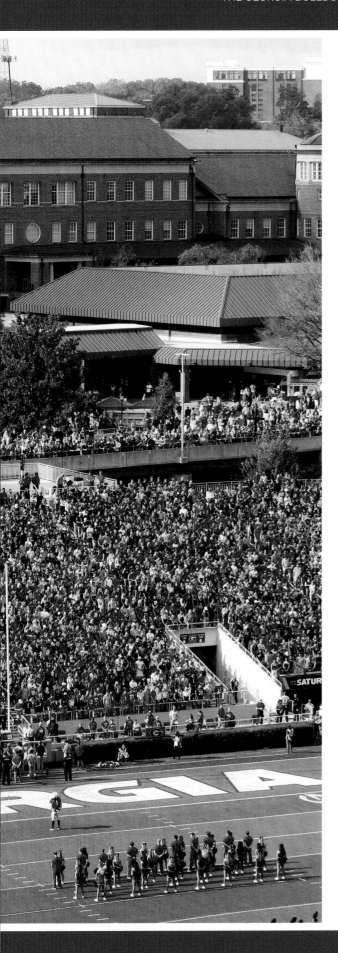

foundation so strong that those of us who inherited it after him ... what an incredible place he made."

Brooks praised Dooley's vision by pointing out that when he became athletic director in 1979, the program had one national title. It came in football in 1942. The university now has 23 national championships, 16 by women's teams, and 78 conference titles because of Dooley's focus and desire to turn the entire athletic department into the best in the NCAA.

Brooks said he tries to follow the two lessons he learned from Dooley: work hard and treat people with respect and kindness.

"Coach Dooley is University of Georgia athletics, and Georgia athletics is coach Dooley," Brooks said.

Morehead highlighted Dooley's insatiable curiosity.

Morehead said a conversation with Dooley would often start with a question: What book are you reading and is it worth me reading? That's not something Morehead said he gets asked a lot. That desire to learn was reflected in Dooley's desire to help many areas of the university, including the library.

One of his books, "Dooley's Playbook: The 34 Most Memorable Plays in Georgia Football History," was on sale at Stegeman Coliseum. Proceeds won't go to athletics, but will instead assist the Redcoat Marching Band, which had members at the celebration.

"Coach Dooley's love of our institution was unwavering, and he worked until the very end, tirelessly, to support this great university," Morehead said. "He will be missed by all of us who had the opportunity to get to know him and love him."

Kemp discussed how Dooley's approach to business and his leadership style influenced him when he was a small-business person.

"His impact went far beyond the hedges," Kemp said. "It transformed the entire athletics department and, in many ways, the whole university itself. When we yell 'Go Dawgs,' we will think of the legacy of Vince Dooley." ■

Former Georgia player Charley Trippi and coach and athletic director Vince Dooley are recognized before the game against Tennessee on November 5, 2022. (Jason Getz/The Atlanta Journal-Constitution)

GEORGIA 37, GEORGIA TECH 14

November 26, 2022 • Athens, Georgia

SENIOR DAY DOMINANCE

Late Dawgs Surge Proves Too Much for Yellow Jackets

By Michael Cunningham

Georgia Tech hadn't put this much pressure on Georgia since 2016. That's the last time the Yellow Jackets beat the Bulldogs – or even led them in a game. The burden was much heavier for the Bulldogs this time around.

In 2016, Georgia was in the first season of its transition from coach Mark Richt to Kirby Smart and had lost four games before playing Tech. For this meeting, Georgia was undefeated, ranked No. 1 and favored by six touchdowns.

The Jackets made the Bulldogs sweat for 40 minutes of game time at Sanford Stadium. Georgia dominated the final 20 by scoring on five consecutive possessions while holding Tech scoreless until garbage time.

In the end, the Bulldogs secured another blowout victory, 37-14, over their in-state rivals. Senior Day wasn't ruined by an unthinkable loss, and Georgia secured back-to-back undefeated regular seasons for the first time since the early 1980s.

"There were some lulls in the game at times and some sleepwalking through it," Smart said. "That always scares you. I thought our fans kind of pushed us over the edge for some momentum in the game."

Georgia fans went home happy about a fifth consecutive victory over the Jackets. Georgia is 18-3 in

the series since Tech won three in a row from 1998-2000.

But before the Bulldogs overwhelmed Tech in the latest installment of "Clean Old-Fashioned Hate" they were stymied by some of their season-long issues.

The Bulldogs sputtered in the red zone and gave up some big pass plays. Penalties pushed them back when they were close to the end and kept Tech drives alive. Kenny McIntosh had a 78-yard reception in the third quarter, but Georgia produced only 57 yards on its 17 other pass attempts.

"We've got to play better in all three phases of the game than we did today if we want to go where we want to go," Smart said.

According to cfbstats.com, the Bulldogs entered the weekend ranked 51st among FBS teams in the percentage of red-zone trips that resulted in a touchdown (66 percent). They made it inside Tech's 20-yard line five times and netted three TDs. The Bulldogs surrendered 14 pass plays of 30-plus yards over their first 11 games. Tech started a third-string quarterback, yet had two pass plays of more than 30 yards.

Those are some of the reasons why Georgia, favored by 36 points, led only 10-7 at halftime.

Said Georgia's Ladd McConkey: "We've played really good halves, but as far as putting a whole game together, we haven't been there completely yet (with) clicking, not

Kendall Milton ran for 56 yards on four carries, including a 44-yard touchdown run. (Jason Getz/The Atlanta Journal-Constitution)

STRONG LEGS WILL RUN THAT
WEAK LEGS MAY WALK
Sic Vos Non Vobis

GOVERNOR'S CUP

Children's Healthcare of Atlanta
Gridiron Classic

turning the ball over and just playing our game. I feel like once we do that, it's going to be awesome."

Georgia allowed a first-quarter touchdown for the first time all season while falling behind 7-0. The Jackets beat Georgia in 2016 here by churning out 226 yards rushing with the triple-option and hitting on some big pass plays. This time, they had the Bulldogs on their heels with a quick-tempo, no-huddle passing attack.

Georgia pretty much shut down the visitors after that. The Jackets made it past midfield twice over their next nine possessions. They'll lament some of the plays they failed to make when they had Georgia in retreat.

A dropped pass by a wide-open receiver would have put Tech at least in field-goal range with a 7-0 lead. Georgia started a drive at its 44-yard line after a targeting penalty against Tech and went on to kick a field goal. The Bulldogs faced third-and-goal at the 5 when Stetson Bennett's pass to Marcus Rosemy-Jacksaint went just over a defender's reach for a TD that gave them the lead for good.

Tech had a chance to tie or go ahead before halftime. The Bulldogs converted a fourth down at Tech's 26-yard line, but a face-mask penalty pushed them out of field-goal range. Georgia downed the punt at the 2-yard line. The Jackets made it to midfield on Zach Gibson's long pass to E.J. Jenkins and gained a first down at UGA's 38 on Gibson's 13-yard scramble.

But that's as far as the Jackets made it before punting. On their first drive after halftime, they botched the snap on a punt attempt to set up Georgia 17 yards from the end zone. Tech stopped Bennett twice on runs near the goal line before he passed to Brock Bowers for a TD on fourth down. Bowers snagged the ball with his fingertips just before it hit the ground.

The Jackets fumbled the ball away on the first play of their next possession. A competitive effort quickly

turned into a rout. The season probably is over for the Jackets after they failed to gain bowl eligibility with a sixth victory, though there is a small chance they could fill a bowl slot at 5-7. They were 4-4 under interim coach Brent Key.

"I didn't see any quit in our guys out there," Key said. "I thought they played their tails off until the clock hit zero. That's something to build (on)."

The Bulldogs have a good chance to become the first back-to-back national champions since Alabama in 2011 and 2012. The Crimson Tide lost a game during each of those seasons. The Bulldogs can do them one better by winning in the SEC Championship game, a CFP semifinal and the national championship game.

Georgia's seniors already are the class with the most wins in program history. They also can boast of making it through the grind of the SEC regular season without a loss in consecutive years.

"It is cool," Bennett said. "We worked for it. But we didn't come into the season trying to go 12-0. We're trying to go 15-0."

To pull that off, the Bulldogs will have to play better than they did against Tech. ∎

Offensive lineman Warren Ericson kisses the Governor's Cup trophy, awarded annually to the winner of the Georgia vs. Georgia Tech matchup. (Hyosub Shin/The Atlanta Journal-Constitution)

DAWGS WITH A CAPITAL 'D'

In Era of Wide-Open Offense, Great Defense Puts Georgia on Top

By Michael Cunningham • November 29, 2022

It wasn't long ago that Georgia was behind the times in big-time college football.

The Bulldogs were trying to win national championships with great defense and a conservative approach on offense. Meanwhile, Alabama, Clemson, Ohio State and LSU were ringing up points on the way to the College Football Playoff. They had wide-open offenses with top NFL prospects at quarterback and the skill positions.

Well, look at what's happened since then.

Those teams still score a lot of points for the most part, while the Bulldogs are relatively ordinary on offense. But Georgia is the best team in the country because no one plays defense like the Bulldogs.

That's been true since the start of last season, and it really has come into focus as CFP contenders faded in recent weeks while capitulating on defense.

Ohio State surrendered 45 points and a program-record 8.8 yards per play to Michigan. South Carolina hung 63 points on Tennessee, which also allowed Bama's offense to score 42.

The Crimson Tide gave up 52 points to Tennessee and 32 against LSU. Clemson allowed 30-plus points three times and lost twice. TCU and (especially) USC just aren't that good on defense.

It's hard to imagine Georgia's defense being that inept. The Bulldogs haven't allowed more than 22 points this season Kent State scored six points in garbage time to reach that mark.

They gave up more than 18 points just once in 2021, to Alabama in the SEC Championship game. Georgia's defense proved that 34-point tally was a one-off by holding Bama to a season-low 18 points in the national title game.

"They're tough-minded, they play physical, they play downhill," LSU coach Brian Kelly said while describing the UGA defense. "We've obviously seen a lot of it (in the SEC), but you've got to make sure you minimize the negative plays against a defense like this. You can get into some bad plays, and now you are behind the chains. They get you to third down, now there's a lot of things they can do."

Georgia's defense shouldn't be so good after so many good players departed following last season. NFL teams selected eight Bulldogs defenders in this year's draft, including five in the first round. Kirby Smart's recruiting is great, but that's a lot of talent and experience to replace.

Yet Georgia's defense is better. I always assume Smart will field a good defense, but even I didn't see that coming.

Georgia is giving up slightly more points per game, 11.3 this season vs. 10.2 last season, but the defense rates higher in Bill Connelly's SP+ metric (adjusted

Georgia lost eight defenders to the 2022 NFL Draft, including five in the first round, but improved in some defensive metrics from the dominant 2021 outfit. (Jason Getz/The Atlanta Journal-Constitution)

for situation, tempo and opponent). The gap between Georgia's defense and an average unit is larger this season, as is the gap between Georgia's defense and the second best (Iowa).

The Bulldogs can make high-scoring offenses look awful. They did it to Alabama in last season's national title game. They've done it to Tennessee in back-to-back years.

Alabama's defense used to be the national standard. Nick Saban's teams never ranked below seventh in defensive SP+ from 2008-20. They were No. 1 in seven of those 13 years. Alabama was ninth in 2021 and 12th so far this season.

Saban revived Bama as a national title contender when he reluctantly accepted that winning big requires opening up the offense. But the Crimson Tide have regressed by their standards because their defense is merely good rather than great. Georgia has nudged ahead of the Tide by being better at keeping teams from scoring.

When Smart's teams have disappointed, much of the talk centered on the offense. The Bulldogs lost the 2018 national championship game to Alabama while scoring 23 points. The next year they were held to 16 points in a loss at LSU. That left them no room for error against Alabama in the SEC Championship game. The Crimson Tide came from behind to win while holding Georgia to seven points after halftime.

In 2019, Georgia scored only 17 points in that weird home loss to South Carolina. The Bulldogs still had a chance to make the CFP that year but lost 37-10 to LSU in the SEC title game. That's when Smart famously declared that the perception he wants to play "man ball" is wrong, it was just that Georgia didn't have the wide receivers necessary to spread opponents out and throw the ball.

What was overlooked in those losses is that, for most of them, Smart's defense wasn't good, either. The thought was that the Bulldogs wouldn't be a true contender until they could win shootouts. What's happened instead is Georgia rarely gets into shootouts because the other team struggles to score.

That's why it's hardly mattered that Georgia's 2022 offense isn't as good as last year's group.

The Bulldogs are scoring about the same number of points per game (38.6 vs. 38.2), but that top-line number flatters them. Georgia's offense slipped from second to 21st in SP+. Much of that decline is because the Bulldogs don't produce as many big plays and finish red-zone trips with TDs less often.

Georgia does score points on 97 percent of its red-zone trips, the best mark in the nation per cfbstats.com. Kicker Jack Podlesny has become even more reliable than predecessor Rodrigo Blankenship, who won the Lou Groza Award in 2019. A good kicker is a great complement to a defense that rarely allows opponents to reach the end zone.

Smart hired Todd Monken to run the offense before last season with good results. Kelly, who faced Georgia twice as Notre Dame coach, said Monken "has got a creative bent to him that's a little bit different than what they had in '17 and '19."

The Bulldogs are better on offense since Monken started calling the plays. That's even though quarterback Stetson Bennett still doesn't have the kind of elite wide receiver that played for every other recent national championship winner.

Bennett and the Bulldogs have a great defense to fall back on when the points aren't plentiful. That's what has Georgia on top in this era of wide-open offensive football. ∎

Defensive back Javon Bullard helped lead a versatile and suffocating defense on the way to a perfect regular season record. (Hyosub Shin/The Atlanta Journal-Constitution)

GEORGIA 50, LSU 30
December 3, 2022 • Atlanta, Georgia

PERFECTLY IMPERFECT
Smart Captures First Win Over LSU as UGA Remains Undefeated
By Chip Towers

With the boogeyman that has been the SEC Championship game vanquished, the Georgia Bulldogs now set their sights on conquering even greater monsters.

The Bulldogs conquered two beasts at once with the 50-30 win over LSU at Mercedes-Benz Stadium. One, they were able to capture the school's first SEC championship since 2017 and only the fourth since divisional play began in 1992. It was the fifth time in the past six years that Georgia has played in the league title game under coach Kirby Smart, but only the second league title during that run.

Two, the Bulldogs were able to put to rest the notion that LSU somehow has their number. The Tigers (9-4), in their first year under coach Brian Kelly, were one of only two SEC teams Smart had never beaten in his seven years as Georgia's coach. He entered the game 0-2 against LSU, last losing 37-10 in the 2019 SEC Championship game (Smart's 0-1 vs. Ole Miss).

"Enough is enough," Georgia running back Kenny McIntosh said afterward. "Kirby's been preaching that to us all week. 'SEC, SEC, SEC — we've got to get the SEC for these seniors.'"

McIntosh is one of those seniors. So is quarterback Stetson Bennett, who was named the game's MVP, and safety Christopher Smith, who made the night's three biggest defensive plays.

It's that subset of Bulldogs that left Smart choking back some emotions during postgame interviews.

"I told those (seniors), I don't want one kid to walk out of our program without an SEC championship ring for their career," Smart said. "That was about to happen if we didn't get this one. They said 'enough was enough' tonight. They got 'em one."

With those anomalies skewered, the Bulldogs can now set their sights on an even greater pursuit – perfection and a back-to-back national championship. Now 13-0, Georgia will face Ohio State in a national semifinal game Dec. 31 in the Chick-fil-A Peach Bowl – its third game at Mercedes-Benz Stadium this season.

As for the perfection piece, LSU is the last team to achieve that in a season, going 15-0 on the way to the 2019 title behind quarterback Joe Burrow and later-to-be-fired coach Ed Orgeron. Meanwhile, the Bulldogs were unable to duplicate that feat after losing to then-No. 3 Alabama in this game last year. They famously vanquished the Bama beast at Lucas Oil Stadium on Jan. 10 to win the national championship.

Georgia was dominant while being far from perfect against LSU. The Bulldogs got 274 yards and four touchdowns on 23-of-29 passing from Bennett – who was named MVP – and a whale of a game from Smith. But considering the offenses that await, there was the rather glaring blemish of allowing 549 yards of

Georgia defensive back Malaki Starks reaches for the ball on what turned out to be a 34-yard touchdown catch for LSU wide receiver Malik Nabers. (Jason Getz/The Atlanta Journal-Constitution)

offense – 502 of which came via the forward pass – to an LSU team that started a hobbled quarterback and played the second half with his backup.

But the Bulldogs countered with some pretty explosive offense of their own, 529 yards total, with 255 rushing, including 113 from Kendall Milton. And with the 50 points, Georgia has scored 99 points in its past two outings in the Falcons' home stadium. Bennett was almost perfect in a 49-3 win over Oregon here to open the season. Not surprisingly, he likes the prospect of possibly getting to play on this field again.

"I don't know what goes into all those decisions," said Bennett, a sixth-year senior who was 19-of-24 passing for 279 yards and four touchdowns, "but, yeah, we like this place."

After a wacky opening period, the Bulldogs settled in for the night with a steamroller of a second quarter. They scored 21 consecutive points before giving Smart some halftime fodder to spew about in the locker room. Georgia's defense allowed the Tigers to drive almost the length of the field in 32 seconds to kick a 42-yard field goal as the buzzer sounded.

Georgia's failing was in letting LSU get loose for 211 yards and notching a first-quarter score behind hobbled quarterback Jayden Daniels. But as the Bulldogs have been wont to do, their defense erased some of its own blemishes with extraordinary plays.

The one that should have turned the game early was a blocked field-goal attempt by Nazir Stackhouse at the end of the Tigers' second possession of the game. The crazy part of it was the ball ended up resting undeterred on the Georgia 4-yard line. Finally, after some coaxing from teammates and coaches, Smith picked up the ball. With many LSU players watching – and some Bulldogs as well – Smith ran the ball untouched 96 yards down the Georgia sideline for a touchdown. With 3:33 remaining in the opening quarter, it gave the Bulldogs a 7-0 lead, but with the Tigers lined up to kick a short field goal, represented a 10-point swing.

LSU answered only 1:12 later with a 7-play, 75-yard drive, which meant it had gone the length of the field on its

Tight end Darnell Washington only had one catch on the day, but it was a timely one with this 14-yard touchdown. (Jason Getz/The Atlanta Journal-Constitution)

first two drives. Georgia would answer, too, and the game suddenly took on the complexion of a shootout.

But on the Tigers' next possession, the senior Smith made another play. He batted away a pass for Jack Bech. The ball ended up bouncing off a fallen Bech's helmet and up into the arms of Georgia linebacker Smael Mondon.

Taking over at the 22, Bennett then hit Ladd McConkey with a strike on a quick post, and the Bulldogs were up 21-7 and the partisan Georgia crowd in The Benz was fully ignited.

The rest of the quarter belonged to Georgia, which would score on two more Bennett passes, including one from three yards out to freshman Dillon Bell with 32 seconds remaining in the half to make the score 35-7.

The second half basically was more of the same, with the Bulldogs seemingly losing focus for short spurts. LSU's Daniels, who came in with a sprained ankle, sat for the rest of the night while his understudy Garrett Nussmeier took over. He exposed for Georgia's playoff opponents this team's defensive weakness – being able to cover good receivers downfield. He, too, hit the Bulldogs with 294 yards and two touchdowns.

"We got a lot of work to do," said Smith, who had an interception, a pass-deflection that led to another turnover and a tackle for loss in addition to the 96-yard touchdown. "We definitely don't flush this. But we were able to come out on top with a great team win. We got to get back to the drawing board and continue to work."

Most of the details were unimportant on this night. This was more of a coronation in between figuring out what teams will be in front of Georgia and its ultimate goal to become the first repeat national champion since Alabama in 2012.

"For me and Chris, it took us a while to get here, right?" said Bennett, speaking of Smith, the fifth-year guy sitting to his right. "There's really no option but to play well now, right? When things start going bad, what are you going to do? ... We knew how hard it was to play for the University of Georgia, right? So now we'll do almost anything to win. I think we have a lot of older guys like that." ∎

Georgia's defense wasn't as stout as normal in the win over LSU, but they were able to bottle up quarterback Jaden Daniels on this play. (Jason Getz/The Atlanta Journal-Constitution)

19

TIGHT END

BROCK BOWERS

A Marvel at Tight End, Bowers Has Overwhelmed Defenses from Day 1

By Gabriel Burns • December 4, 2022

Brock Bowers might be the best individual offensive player among the four teams in the College Football Playoff. The Georgia tight end is a marvel, an athletic mismatch at a position at which he has no equal.

Yet in the two relatively competitive games before the SEC Championship game, Bowers had seven catches for 30 yards and a score. It could be suggested the Bulldogs were saving him for their tougher battles.

"I'm not sure, I don't make the plan," Bowers said with a chuckle when proposed that theory.

The truth is Georgia, rich with offensive options and never desperate for a single play, simply didn't need Bowers' brilliance to beat Kentucky or Georgia Tech. As the tight end himself noted, "We have a bunch of playmakers. Why not give them all the ball?"

But the Bulldogs will need Bowers – the winner of the Mackey Award presented to the best tight end in college football – against Ohio State in the national semifinals. And they used the SEC title game to announce his return to prominence.

Bowers had six catches for 81 yards and a touchdown in the 50-30 win against LSU. He was involved early, helping Georgia build a 25-point halftime lead. Each time the Bulldogs looked in his direction, he showed the audience why he was perhaps the best talent on a field full of it.

During their first touchdown drive, Bulldogs quarterback Stetson Bennett hit Bowers for 15- and 32-yard gains. Bowers scored a 3-yard touchdown easily when Bennett rolled out and found Bowers as he separated from defenders.

"It's always fun catching the ball," Bowers said. "I'm just trying to do my job, do as much as I can with the ball in my hands."

Up 21-7, Georgia assembled a 13-play drive just before half that included a third-and-3 conversion by Bowers in the red zone. Two plays later, Bennett found his other beastly tight end Darnell Washington for a touchdown. Bowers had five catches for 58 yards at the break.

As the third quarter wound down and it appeared

Tight end Brock Bowers is one of the best offensive players in college football, winning the Mackey Award presented to the best tight end in 2022. (Jason Getz/The Atlanta Journal-Constitution)

the Bulldogs again had disregarded their top weapon, Bennett fired a tight-window throw to Bowers, whose catch-and-run accounted for 23 yards. The Bulldogs scored on that drive and reached the 50-point mark. Bowers' catch came on the team's final pass of the game (sans a two-point conversion attempt).

It's arguable that Bowers is Georgia's most talented player – defensive tackle Jalen Carter might have that distinction – but there are few, if any, skill players among the CFP candidates who possess Bowers' rare ability.

Ohio State has skill talents such as Marvin Harrison and Jaxon Smith-Njigba, should he return from injury. TCU has receiver Quentin Johnston, whom you'll find in the first round of any 2023 mock draft. The Wolverines had running back Blake Corum, but he's out following knee surgery. They still have impressive players such as running back Donovan Edwards and receiver Ronnie Bell.

Harrison is the only one in Bowers' talent class. The national scene is well-aware of Georgia's preposterously deep tight end group, and Bowers is the headliner. But despite his renowned name, he hasn't always been the focal point of the offense.

The reason: He hasn't needed to be. That's the case when you win 12 of 13 games by double digits. He's eclipsed 100 yards receiving only twice – half as many occasions as 2021. His nine touchdowns are three fewer than last season.

"If we're winning – we're 13-0 – and if we keep winning, then I don't have a problem with who's getting the ball or if I get any catches at all," Bowers said. "As long as we're winning. We came here to win games."

Bowers is conducive to doing just that. The Bulldogs will unleash him when needed. Last season, he had 139 yards in the SEC Championship game, which Georgia lost to Alabama.

He had nine catches for 91 yards across the ensuing two CFP games, scoring in both as the Bulldogs won the championship (a humorous tidbit: Bowers said celebrating the SEC title was "nicer" than the national championship because he was immediately drug-tested following the latter while his teammates celebrated).

Bowers has drawn attention nearly every week for his highlight plays, but he never exceeded five catches in a single contest during the regular season. He crossed 70 yards receiving only twice. He had over 100 total yards on three occasions.

Then, in the most important game to date, Bowers was the team's leading receiver with a season-best six catches. Georgia's offense is better than last season's, as its 50-point outburst reminded spectators. Bowers tormenting the minds of opposing defenders and coordinators is a large part of the equation, even when the surface stats are forgettable.

Players aren't supposed to be so nuanced, speedy and well-built, especially at age 19. The Bulldogs plucked this behemoth from Napa, California, and he's overwhelmed defenses from Day 1. Talents such as Bowers are what totally separates Georgia from the pack.

"If you look at him, he has like 8 percent body fat," Washington said. "It's crazy to see as a tight end. And everybody knows he's fast. He's just a unique guy."

Bet on Bowers further asserting himself in the CFP. Defenses will try to contain him, but he hasn't been tamed when Georgia has truly needed him. Many already consider him the greatest tight end in Bulldogs history.

Just as there's no doubt Georgia is No. 1, there's no question Bowers is America's best collegiate tight end – even if he won't accept the flattery. "I just feel like I have a lot to prove," Bowers said. "I just have to keep working." ∎

Georgia utilizes Brock Bowers selectively, spreading the ball around in blowout wins, yet leaning on him more heavily in the biggest matchups. (Jason Getz/The Atlanta Journal-Constitution)

13
QUARTERBACK

STETSON BENNETT

Georgia's Heisman Finalist Proves to Be Professional Odds Conqueror

By Gabriel Burns • December 9, 2022

There was Stetson Bennett, pride of Blackshear and idol of Athens, eating chicken parmesan with his family at Tony's in Midtown Manhattan. For just a lunch, he was like everybody else.

It was a scarce moment of normalcy for the national champion-turned Heisman Trophy finalist. It was his second time in New York City, but his first time visiting since becoming one of the more memorable college football players in history.

Just as it seemed his story couldn't grow grander, it lands on Broadway.

"It means a lot; it means we have a really good team, that a lot of other people did a lot of things so that I could play well," Bennett said. "It is kind of crazy just to be up here. I walked on (at Georgia). I am glad that you guys (media) are here, a bunch of familiar faces at least. I get homesick.

"It's crazy and it's special. I'm excited to see what this whole thing is."

By now, his underdog tale is common literature. Most everyone knows of Bennett, the undersized unknown from South Georgia who was part of Georgia's 2017 recruiting class. They know how he was the scout-team Baker Mayfield ahead of that unforgettable Rose Bowl victory. They know how much he and his family love Georgia, how much coach Kirby Smart has trusted him.

They know how Bennett once left Athens only to return. They know how he was benched "I was not good enough," Bennett said in reflection. They know how he outdueled higher touted players en route to becoming a national champion. They even laughed during his much-talked-about "Good Morning America" appearance the morning after roasting Alabama in a title-clinching fourth quarter.

Once again, Bennett has defied convention. Some were surprised by his inclusion in this group, but there's no play of which he's more accustomed than "Deliver when I'm disregarded." His Heisman candidacy is a microcosm of his football life. Bennett not only continuously surpasses expectations – that's on him, but he consistently surprises as he does – that's on others.

Stetson Bennett calls a play over center Sedrick Van Pran during Georgia's 26-22 win against Missouri. (Jason Getz/ The Atlanta Journal-Constitution)

This time, he's up for college football's greatest individual honor at age 25.

"I never really entertained the thought," Bennett said of becoming a Heisman finalist. He did credit Bulldogs offensive quality-control coach Buster Faulkner, who mentioned the possibility before the season.

"We've thrown the ball more this year, for whatever reason," Bennett said. "We're scoring more points this year. So far, it's been more explosive. There has been more asked of me this year, which has been fun for me. I've enjoyed it a lot. I think that comes from me earning it, me being good enough to do that. I don't think I necessarily was last year. Some spots, but not all the time."

Bennett was born in 1997; so was Lamar Jackson, who won the Heisman in 2016 and was NFL MVP in 2019, and Kyler Murray, who won the Heisman in 2018. Bennett is four months and 10 days older than Justin Herbert, who's considered a budding star quarterback in his third NFL season. Bennett is older than two former Alabama quarterbacks, Jalen Hurts and Tua Tagovailoa, who both are 24 and leading likely NFL playoff teams.

During the ages when most Heisman winners achieved glory, Bennett simply was trying to stick around. Bennett's path is relatable to anyone, unlike, say, the rise of a LeBron James, Bryce Harper or Peyton Manning. Those players were anointed as teenagers and met their hype. Bennett, as a teenager, was quietly setting state high-school records, but his physical build let him slip through the cracks.

That only began what was a challenging college career until Bennett secured the starting job in September 2021.

"Stetson, you can tell every time that something tough has come in his life, he's stepped up to the plate and took it, put his chin up and his chest out," said Ohio State quarterback C.J. Stroud, fellow Heisman finalist and opponent for Georgia in the Peach Bowl. "You can't do anything but respect that. I tip my hat to him.

"At the end of the day, that's a hard road to go on. I've been on it myself, where a lot of people don't believe in

Stetson Bennett completes a pass to running back Kenny McIntosh during a 33-0 rout of Samford in September. (Curtis Compton/The Atlanta Journal-Constitution)

you. They tell you that you're crazy and your dreams probably won't work out. But to be honest, if people aren't telling you that, then your dreams probably aren't big enough. I tip my hat to him and wish much success and health to him."

Bennett's recruiting ranking is irrelevant now, as are his pro prospects. He just capped his second consecutive undefeated regular season with Georgia, this time adding an SEC championship. Georgia has lost one game over the past two years under Bennett. This season, it won every contest by double digits except at Missouri, where they might hang a banner for staying so close.

Keeping with the theme, there still are plenty of Bennett skeptics. Some opine he wasn't the best player on his team or his offense, so why is he in New York?

"It probably keeps me humble," Bennett said. "I don't go into a workout with a copy of a tweet, but … It's probably like a culture thing. Those thousands of 'not good enoughs' seeped into my brain. And I can say, 'You're not there yet.' Because I remember what it was like to not be there then, and it did kind of suck, so now, it's just in my (brain) to keep going, 'We're still not there yet.'"

None of the criticism is within Bennett's control. Here's what is: He's maximized himself during the past two years. He wasn't flawless this season, as he'd tell you. Georgia's margin for error was wider than the Hudson. But when the Bulldogs needed Bennett, he provided.

Georgia's three biggest games came against Oregon, Tennessee and LSU. Bennett ripped through the Ducks' defense on opening weekend, leading Georgia to a 49-3 win that aged well as Oregon ascended. Tennessee came to Athens as the No. 1 team. Georgia destroyed the Volunteers 27-13 with Bennett outplaying then-Heisman front-runner Hendon Hooker.

In the SEC Championship game, Bennett was sharp yet again. He led an offensive showcase won by Georgia 50-30 over an LSU team that defeated reigning Heisman winner Bryce Young and Alabama weeks earlier.

Bennett's cumulative stats across those three contests: 65-of-85 passing for 899 yards, 10 touchdowns (eight passing) and no interceptions.

"My uncle told me," Bennett said, pausing for a moment before stressing he wanted to get the message right. "He told me, 'If you don't have any choice, it's easy.' So figure out a way."

Bennett isn't the favorite for the award. But he has his eyes on another trophy, anyway. And as illustrious as the Heisman is, becoming a back-to-back national-champion quarterback for your childhood team is even more prestigious.

But first, this pitstop in New York City. A weekend of fine dining and schmoozing before he spills ink on The Book of Bennett's final page. ∎

Stetson Bennett has delivered indisputable results as Georgia's quarterback and was honored as a Heisman Trophy finalist in 2022. (Jason Getz/The Atlanta Journal-Constitution)

TAKE A BOW

The Long Roads to All-American for Jalen Carter and Christopher Smith

By Chip Towers • December 13, 2022

The Georgia Bulldogs were well represented during awards season, which followed their 2022 unbeaten regular season.

It could be argued the Bulldogs didn't rack up to the extent one might think for the nation's No. 1-ranked and undefeated team. Georgia had four players on The Associated Press All-America team. Alabama, by comparison, had five.

For years, the AP collection has stood as the most respected and appreciated group in college football. This year, it featured Georgia first-teamers Jalen Carter and Christopher Smith. Brock Bowers and Jamon Dumas-Johnson were placed on the second team.

Being named a first-team All-American is a notable accomplishment on its own, but the journeys of Carter and Smith to land there are particularly incredible considering the circumstances.

First, neither became a starter until their junior seasons. Carter bided his time behind future NFL first-rounders Devonte Wyatt and Jordan Davis, then missed most or all of six games in the middle of Georgia's schedule this year because of ankle and knee injuries.

Smith came to Athens from Atlanta as a cornerback, then fell back on the depth chart as he transitioned to safety and toiled behind Richard LeCounte and J.R. Reed for two seasons. Smith's first start didn't come until the last half of his junior season in 2020 after LeCounte was sidelined by injuries sustained in a motorcycle crash. He has rarely come off the field since.

Both players have stood out in a big way these past two years as Georgia pushes to become the first back-to-back national champion in a decade.

Smith, a graduate of Hapeville Charter School, has started all 13 games this season, leads the Bulldogs with three interceptions and ranks fourth on the teams in tackles with 50. In the SEC Championship game victory over LSU, Smith returned a blocked field-goal attempt 96 yards for a touchdown, intercepted a pass, deflected another pass that resulted in an interception and recorded three tackles, including one for a loss

Smith captured national attention for his heads-up return of the blocked kick. But it was jumping the route of an LSU tight end which resulted in the ball caroming off the player's helmet and into the hands of linebacker Smael Mondon for an interception that set up a Georgia score that most impressed coach Kirby Smart. It was the same route that Smith jumped for

Defensive back Christopher Smith tackles Ohio State wide receiver Xavier Johnson during the Peach Bowl. Smith and teammate Jalen Carter were named first-team All-Americans. (Jason Getz/The Atlanta Journal-Constitution)

a 79-yard touchdown return against Clemson in the opening game of the 2021 season.

"It's more about his instincts," Smart said of Smith. "He jumped (the route). He played it aggressive. He understood what the quarterback's check was. He understood his leverage. ... He saw it, jumped it, and by him jumping, it caused the ball to go in the air."

Despite starting only seven games, Carter has 29 tackles, including seven tackles for loss and three sacks. He has two forced fumbles and recorded 25 quarterback pressures. Over the past six games, he has accounted for 24 tackles, 6.5 TFLs, three sacks and a pair of forced fumbles. His signature moment came in the SEC Championship game when he sacked LSU quarterback Jayden Daniels and lifted him off the ground with his left arm while flashing the No. 1 sign with his right hand.

Both players were up for other national individual awards but did not win. Smith was a finalist for the Bronko Nagurski Award, while Carter was a Lombardi Award finalist. Last week, Carter and Smith were named to the Walter Camp Football Foundation and Football Writers Association of America (FWAA) All-American first team, while Bowers made the FWAA first team and Walter Camp second team. ∎

Christopher Smith pressures Florida quarterback Anthony Richardson during Georgia's 42-20 win. The Bulldogs won nearly every regular-season contest by double-digit margins in 2022, a testament to their elite defense. (Jason Getz/The Atlanta Journal-Constitution)

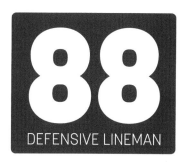

88
DEFENSIVE LINEMAN

JALEN CARTER

There is Nothing Quiet About the Way Jalen Carter Plays Football

By Gabriel Burns • December 30, 2022

Georgia's Jalen Carter seems to decide games on his terms, as if his team's victory is a simple switch away.

In 2019, coach Jeff Rolson returned to Apopka County High School hoping he would keep the program an Orlando, Florida-area powerhouse. His first exhibition was a spring jamboree in which Apopka faced two separate Jacksonville schools in two halves.

In the first half against Atlantic Coast, the Darters appeared pedestrian. "What have I got myself into? We don't look like much," Rolson recalled.

The second half against Raines was a different outcome. Carter, a senior, was the engineer.

"It was like a switch got flipped," Rolson said. "Our whole team, led by Jalen, exploded, particularly defensively. That was a half of football that I'll always remember because he was just superior in every way: stopping the run, rushing the passer, sacks, multiple hits on the quarterback.

"We've had NFL players. I've seen NFL players. I've never seen a kid dominating like he dominated. ... He could just take over a game. If he decided it was time, he was unblockable."

Apopka later lost the state championship game on a two-point conversion. But Carter continued his ascent as one of the more coveted recruits in the country. These days, he's flipping switches in the national championship game last season against Alabama or against then-No. 1 Tennessee in November.

Carter is Georgia's best player. He might've been last season, too, when the Bulldogs had five first-round NFL draft selections. The only question about Carter, whom quarterback Stetson Bennett recently called "superman," is whether he's the best player in America.

The last time we saw this behemoth, he sacked LSU quarterback Jayden Daniels late in the first half of the SEC Championship game as Georgia distanced itself. The play's result wasn't as relevant as what it represented.

Carter, after discarding offensive linemen like used tissue, corralled Daniels and hoisted him like a trophy. Carter held Daniels aloft in his left arm as he flashed the No. 1 sign with his right hand.

There perhaps is no better moment to illustrate Georgia's place in college football – and Carter's. What a beautiful statue it would make, a monument to this time so cherished by Bulldogs fanatics.

Jalen Carter has been turning heads throughout his career, from Apopka County High School in Florida to college football's biggest stage. (Jason Getz/The Atlanta Journal-Constitution)

"In high school on Fridays, I'd send him my little pep text message, and I still do it every Saturday morning," said Toni Brown, Carter's mother. "That morning, I said, 'Jalen, you better get to that quarterback.' And I probably said you better lay him on his back or something. I didn't say put one finger up in the air.

"I asked him, 'Jalen, what did that mean?' He was like, 'I was telling you I got him.' I was super proud of that moment and the way he handled the situation and did not just sack that quarterback and lay him on his back, which is like what I probably said."

During an era when Georgia always seems better, there's no one who has perfected their art like the pride of Apopka. Carter's hulking dominance hasn't been secret. It simply has been subdued when Carter joined the Bulldogs as the No. 18 prospect nationally, per 247Sports Composite rankings, in the 2020 class. He was a part-time player because of Georgia's defensive riches.

Defensive linemen Travon Walker, Devonte Wyatt and Jordan Davis all were first-round NFL draft picks in 2022. Carter was selectively mixed in. He led SEC interior rushers with a 13.6 percent pressure rate last season.

Wyatt promised Carter will be "amazing." Walker, who was drafted No. 1 overall, said during ESPN's broadcast of Georgia's spring game that Carter is "a force to be reckoned with."

"Those guys motivated me to do more," Carter said in April. "They told me I could be a top-10 pick."

Bulldogs coach Kirby Smart emphasized Carter's conditioning in spring with an increased snap count looming. Smart: "The talent is oozing. It's a matter of: Can he play every play with maximum intensity and be able to sustain it?"

Eight months later, the answer is "yes," even though Carter dealt with injuries. He hurt his ankle in the season opener against Oregon and sustained an MCL sprain a few weeks later against Missouri.

Carter missed a month before returning limited against Florida. Finally, when Georgia hosted top-ranked Tennessee in early November, he was unleashed.

The results: four tackles, two tackles for loss, two forced fumbles, one sack and one shell-shocked Volunteers offense that appeared immortal entering that fateful Saturday. Georgia had six sacks after having 10 across its previous eight contests. Pro Football Focus graded Carter's performance a 92.3, his career-best outing by its metric.

Teammates genuflect to Carter's impact. The tour de force against Tennessee encapsulated his value. Even when he's not compiling the numbers – he has only three sacks – he's creating them for others.

Carter exceeded 40 snaps in only the national championship game last season. Since playing 48 snaps against the Volunteers, he's played 40, 46, 45 and 45, respectively, to close this season.

He played 141 snaps from Week 9 through the conference championship last season. He's logged 243 snaps over that same period this season. Carter has proved, even in a season interrupted by injury, he's worthy of larger responsibilities.

Carter keeps a low profile off the field. He's spoken with reporters once in college. He isn't a showman. His one public appearance: returning to Apopka in August to host a youth football camp.

"It takes a village to raise a child," Brown said. "The entire community, the entire city of Apopka, has been my village. They supported us then, and to this day they still do."

Those around Carter describe him as quiet with a good sense of humor. "He's a funny guy, always joking around," teammate Smael Mondon said. He's a change

Kentucky place kicker Matt Ruffolo attempts a field goal as Georgia defensive linemen Jalen Carter and Warren Brinson try to block the attempt. (Jason Getz/The Atlanta Journal-Constitution)

of pace from Wyatt's and Davis' gigantic personalities. Carter's demeanor apparently already is a talking point.

ESPN draft analyst Todd McShay recently mentioned Carter potentially having "character issues." He didn't elaborate further, but teammates dismissed the comments. Defensive tackle Zion Logue: "A lot of guys were just laughing at it. They don't know the real him." The NFL will dive into every detail down to Carter's preferred cologne, so the discussion will continue.

"He has the heart of gold," Brown said. "Nobody could say harsh things about him. When we heard the comment, I really had to listen to it and make sure that they were talking about my Jalen.

"But I understand the logistics and the things that happen and how it goes. And I know this is one of many comments that are not true that are going to come out about him. So our focus is just to make sure that his head is on strong and he does not let any of that interfere with him. He is a big teddy bear. He loves children. He's a big kid at heart himself."

McShay's colleague Mel Kiper, the long-time scouting guru (if there is such a thing), has Carter ranked No. 1 overall on his board. While a quarterback is likely favored to go first – for the same reason that they've hijacked the Heisman Trophy – Carter should get consideration. Even with the quarterback hoopla, Carter should go in the top five.

Carter has been compared with NFL veteran Fletcher Cox and up-and-comer Quinnen Williams. He'll strive for a career like another Apopka High product, Warren Sapp, who was one of the great interior rushers in NFL history.

"Obviously, I think their careers you could parallel (at this stage)," Rolson said. "Warren did it in the NFL, too, so I wouldn't disrespect him and say that Jalen is going to be what he was. Could he? Yes. But we'll see."

That's a high bar. Carter's ability means it's not an impossible one to reach. Like Sapp, Carter played some tight end, among everything else, at Apopka. Like Sapp, Carter's athletic ability seems preposterous for a man blessed with such a build.

"A kid with that size, strength, speed, explosiveness," Rolson said. "He was throwing down windmill dunks and catching footballs. He punted for us. He could do anything. Literally anything. He could've played middle linebacker, tailback, tight end. There was no hiding it. You knew. The only thing that would keep him from being successful would be (himself) or (an) injury."

Carter's versatility has continued in the SEC, where he's played fullback, tight end and on special teams. He changed the national title game when he blocked Alabama's field-goal attempt.

NFL teams won't ask for so much flair. There's no need being a renaissance man when your premier skill is paramount. Carter can get to the quarterback from anywhere. Evaluators and coaches have preferences in quarterbacks, receivers, cornerbacks, but what Carter offers is universally adorned.

There are few professional players who can even be theorized like him. Aaron Donald, whose timely quarterback hit made the Rams Super Bowl LVI champions, is the modern best-case outcome.

Donald flipped the switch and decided the result that Sunday evening, just as Carter's block against the Crimson Tide might've altered that outcome. Carter aims for an encore in the coming weeks.

"I've heard this since Jalen stepped foot on a football field at the age of 6," Brown said. "I'd always heard 'Hey, he's special. Hey, he's definitely going to the NFL.' Even as his mom, some of the things that he has done, I'm like, 'Oh my goodness, he's definitely going to be a professional athlete' sometimes. So I always thought it for 20 years. And now it's coming to pass." ∎

Jalen Carter leaps over the Mississippi State line in an attempt to block a field goal by place kicker Massimo Biscardi. (Jason Getz/The Atlanta Journal-Constitution)

GEORGIA 42, OHIO STATE 41
December 31, 2022 • Atlanta, Georgia

FOURTH QUARTER MAGIC
UGA Stuns Ohio State to Reach Championship Game
By Chip Towers

The Georgia Bulldogs are heading to Cali. Again. Five years after Georgia started its ascent under coach Kirby Smart with a trip to the Rose Bowl, the Bulldogs are headed west again to play for the college football playoff championship Jan. 9 against TCU. Georgia earned its title-game berth with a stunning 42-41 Peach Bowl win over Ohio State in one semifinal while TCU defeated Michigan 51-45 in the other semifinal held at the Fiesta Bowl.

The Bulldogs are getting back after yet another miraculous comeback engineered by quarterback Stetson Bennett. His touchdown pass to Adonai "A.D." Mitchell with 54 seconds to play gave Georgia a 42-41 lead after it had trailed for most of the game. Mitchell scored the go-ahead TD when the Bulldogs defeated Alabama for the national championship last January.

"Emotionally, it takes a lot out of you to win a game like that," Smart said. "It was an emotional roller coaster out there."

Playing in the semifinals for the third time since that initial appearance in 2017, Georgia advances to the final for the third time – and the first time via the Chick-fil-A Peach Bowl. In keeping with the triplicate theme, it is the third victory this season at Mercedes-Benz Stadium for the Bulldogs (14-0). A record crowd of 79,330 packed in to see it.

The Bulldogs matched their school record for wins in a season set during last year's run to the national championship. Now Georgia will seek to become the first repeat champion in the playoff era and the first in college football since Alabama did it in 2011-12.

"They're defending national champions, they're undefeated, they're a great team," Ohio State coach Ryan Day said. "But there's not one guy in our locker room doesn't think we should've won the game."

After Bennett's 10-yard TD pass to Mitchell completed a five-play, 72-yard scoring drive, Georgia's defense had to stop Ohio State and quarterback C.J. Stroud, which it didn't very often throughout the night.

Stroud did what he does, scrambling and completing passes to get the Buckeyes down to Georgia's 31. But Ohio State would lose a yard, and Stroud threw two incompletions. So Buckeyes kicker Noah Ruggles was left with a 50-yard attempt, which he hooked badly to the left.

Ruggles had made a 48-yarder earlier in the second half. Georgia's Jack Podlesny missed two field-goal attempts but made two as well.

Bennett, who also had a 76-yard touchdown pass to Arian Smith in the fourth quarter, finished with 398 yards and three touchdowns on 23-of-34 passing. He also had an interception.

"If we were going to win this game, we just couldn't give up those explosive plays," Day said.

Running back Kenny McIntosh gets by Ohio State safety Ronnie Hickman for a 52-yard run during the second quarter. (Jason Getz/The Atlanta Journal-Constitution)

Stroud, who finished third in Heisman Trophy voting – one spot ahead of Bennett – had 348 yards on 23-of-34 passing and four TDs.

Georgia was nothing if not resilient. Looking dead in the water trailing by 11 with 8:51 left, Bennett propelled them back into the game with a 76-yard touchdown pass to Smith on the first play from scrimmage. The Bulldogs didn't hesitate in going for the two-point conversion, and it was successful on Bennett's throw to Ladd McConkey. That got Georgia to within 38-35 with 8:41 to play.

It looked as though the Buckeyes might salt away the game after they managed to drive down for a field goal. But that left Bennett with one more chance.

"At the end of the game, I don't know, it kind of frees you up," Bennett said of his penchant for making winning plays. "You've just got to, otherwise we're going to lose."

It was anybody's ballgame after a first half that saw the Buckeyes score late to carry a 28-24 lead into the locker room. But the Bulldogs got the ball first to start the second half after hitting the Buckeyes for 313 yards in the first. Control of the game was still up for grabs.

Georgia went three and out.

Ohio State answered with a six-play, five-pass scoring drive that ended with a 10-yard TD pass to Emeka Egbuka to extend the lead to 35-24 and give the Buckeyes the most points scored against Georgia's storied defense all season.

The Bulldogs punted again.

Georgia would finally get the defensive stop it so badly needed and a 22-yard punt return by Kearis Jackson to boot. So the Bulldogs took over at the Ohio State 32.

They would lose 2 yards in four plays, then Podlesny missed a 52-yard field-goal attempt, his second miss of the night.

When the Buckeyes answered with another pass-happy scoring drive – this one ending in a chip-shot field goal, it felt as though all momentum was on the Ohio State sideline.

Georgia came back from a 21-7 deficit that represented its largest all season to take its first lead of the game, 24-21, on a 32-yard Podlesny field goal with just 1:44 remaining in the first half. Things were looking good for the Bulldogs at that moment because the Buckeyes were out of timeouts.

Turns out they didn't need any.

Four Stroud completions to three different receivers covered the 75 yards with plenty of time to spare. Stroud's second completion to Xavier Johnson on the drive resulted in a 37-yard touchdown and put Ohio State back on top, 28-24.

Georgia's Bennett was nearly picked off by Cameron Brown on a second-down pass from his own 25. The Bulldogs, getting the ball first to start the second half, scrapped the idea of advancing the football at that point and took a knee to let the quarter end.

The halftime numbers were alarming to both defenses, but especially to the one from Georgia that had been so stingy all season. The Buckeyes lit them up with 248 yards, all but 10 coming through the air. Stroud was good on 15 of 19 passes and threw three touchdowns.

Bennett was pretty good, too, completing 12 of 19 passes for 191 yards and a score. But he also threw an interception. The primary difference was the Bulldogs could run the football. They had 122 yards at the half, with Kenny McIntosh getting 52 of his 56 on one run. ■

Wide receiver Arian Smith catches a 76-yard touchdown during the fourth quarter as Georgia mounted a memorable comeback. (Jason Getz/The Atlanta Journal-Constitution)

BENNETT'S BEST

Georgia QB Directs Stunning Fourth-Quarter Comeback

By Ken Sugiura

Up and down for much of the game, Georgia quarterback Stetson Bennett saved his best for last.

With his team down 11 points with nine minutes remaining, Bennett directed the Bulldogs to touchdowns on back-to-back possessions and lifted Georgia to a 42-41 win over Ohio State in an unforgettable Chick-fil-A Peach Bowl matchup at Mercedes-Benz Stadium.

In the final minutes of their College Football Playoff semifinal, in which the Bulldogs had squandered scoring chances, suffered from injuries to starters and often appeared to have cost themselves a chance to play for a second consecutive national championship, Bennett led a comeback from a 38-24 deficit early in the fourth quarter by directing three drives that produced 18 points and survived the Buckeyes' last-second failed field-goal try from 50 yards to secure victory for Georgia.

Bennett, a former walk-on whose journey at Georgia is a story that needs little embellishment, added a most memorable chapter in front of a capacity crowd hanging on every momentum change.

Down 38-27 with 8:51 to play in the fourth quarter, Bennett connected with receiver Arian Smith on a 76-yard touchdown pass on the first play of the drive and then hit receiver Ladd McConkey on the two-point try that cut the lead to 38-35. It was the third catch of the game, but only the sixth of the season for Smith, who ran a double move that caused safety Lathan Ransom to lose his footing.

"That one was just run fast, and he did, and he made the dude fall," Bennett said. "Dude can do things that people can't do. He can run like people can't run, and he can go get the ball."

After Noah Ruggles' field goal with 2:43 left nudged Ohio State's lead back to 41-35, the stage was set for the Bulldogs either to claim glory and keep their national-title quest alive or to see their season end with their first defeat since the SEC Championship game in December 2021.

Huddled before the start of the series, the Bulldogs were fully aware of the stakes. Bennett said that he didn't necessarily remember what words were said.

"But just looking at everybody and saying, 'All right, hey, we haven't played our best, and we haven't done our jobs to the best of our ability, but we're here now. It's in our hands now,'" Bennett said. "'Defense stood up whenever we needed them to. Where else would you rather be? Having the ball with two minutes left, and if you score a touchdown, you win the game.'"

"I looked around, and there was just a whole bunch of just determined, strong stares from all the dudes," he continued. "It gave me confidence, and everybody else had confidence when we went down the field."

That Georgia was in a position to rescue the

game was a bit of fortune. By the Bulldogs' own acknowledgement, they had not played their best. Bennett himself had started out hot, completing nine of his first 10 passes to seven targets, but was off of his game after that. His 11th throw, a second-quarter interception from the Georgia 25-yard line, set up an Ohio State touchdown for a 21-7 lead.

Coming out of halftime down 28-24, the Bulldogs gained one first down in their first three possessions of the second half, the last of which started at the Ohio State 32 and produced only a field-goal try that Jack Podlesny missed from 50 yards, his second miss of the game.

It appeared the door was closing on Georgia on its fourth drive of the second half, which at first appeared over when a Bennett pass to tight end Brock Bowers on a fourth-and-6 from the Ohio State 13 was judged short of the marker, giving the ball back to Ohio State.

"I thought the whole stadium thought we didn't get it, and then they reviewed it," Bennett said. "Brock was pretty dumbfounded because he was like, 'I think I got it.'"

Bennett was likeminded. And even when the replay review gave the Bulldogs a first down and new life, Bennett botched the opportunity when he short-armed a lateral to McConkey that fell to the ground, requiring McConkey to dive on the ball to retain possession and resulting in a 10-yard loss.

"Stupid," Bennett said.

Bennett's third-and-goal pass into the end zone from the 13 to McConkey was incomplete into heavy coverage, resulting in Georgia settling for a Podlesny 31-yard field goal that kept Ohio State's lead at two scores, 38-27.

"We didn't play our best game, starting with me," Bennett said.

It was perhaps with that recognition of their serendipitous position that the Bulldogs steeled themselves for their game-winning drive. Starting at their 28-yard line with 2:36 left in the game, Bennett and the Bulldogs got to work. On the second play of the drive, he threw a dart on second-and-8 from the Georgia 30 to Bowers for a 15-yard gain. On a first-and-5 from midfield, he found Kearis Jackson down the seam for a 35-yard gain.

Bennett finished the drive by threading a 10-yard touchdown pass to receiver Adonai Mitchell with 54 seconds remaining. The score and Podlesny's point-after kick gave Georgia its 42-41 lead.

On the play, Mitchell released to the inside before bending his route to the sideline, giving Bennett room for a delivery that electrified Mercedes-Benz Stadium.

On the two fourth-quarter touchdown drives, including the two-point conversion play, Bennett was 7-for-7 passing for 146 yards, two touchdowns and the two-point conversion, using six different targets.

"It's the same thing with everything," Bennett said. "The more you do it, the more comfortable you get. We rep a lot of two minutes. We know what calls we're going to do. We've got players who study the game plan. So it's less so confidence in what I can do. I know that they're going to be where they're going to be and they're going to win their matchups. So all I've got to do is give them the ball."

Bennett finished the game 23-for-34 passing for a career-high 398 yards, three touchdowns and the lone interception. More than the numbers, what will probably linger far longer in the memory of Bennett, his teammates and Georgia fans everywhere is the feeling. At the post-game news conference, Bennett was asked if he had ever played in a game like this one against Ohio State.

"That game was, that was a good game," he said. "I'm looking at these stats right here, and they're pretty much dead even across the board. No, that was special." ■

EPILOGUE

By Brandon Adams

Georgia's second straight national championship will bring about a lot of changes, and the biggest change of all may be the story we tell ourselves about our favorite team.

Since the Bulldogs finished off their perfect season in Los Angeles, in the shadow of Hollywood, let's use the language of movies to explain.

Sports fans like to think of their team as the heroes. They see them as the good guys fighting against evil forces who would try to steal their joy. So, when UGA won the national championship for the first time in more than 40 years last season by knocking off longtime nemesis, Alabama, it may have felt like Luke Skywalker and his friends blowing up the Death Star in Star Wars.

So, UGA's repeat championship this year probably feels more like the original Star Wars movie's first sequel, The Empire Strikes Back. Now, with the Bulldogs in the opposite role. The Empire Strikes Back was the rare movie in which the bad guys won, and while that might be an unusual narrative for films, it's all too common in sports.

Sports fans in Georgia know this. They've seen empires strike back on their favorite teams more times than they can stand.

Whether it was the Falcons failing to hold onto a 28-3 lead against the Patriots in the Super Bowl in 2017 or the Braves coughing up a 2-0 series lead to the Yankees in the 1996 World Series, greedy dynasties have robbed us of our moment more than once.

Georgia has had to deal with this, too. How many heartbreaking losses have there been to Nick Saban's Alabama over the years when victory for the Bulldogs was all but certain — right up until the moment it wasn't?

Those were painful experiences for fans, but they came with an odd form of comfort. Our team may not have won, but at least we know we're the good guys. After all, there's no way a team like the Yankees or the Patriots or certainly Alabama could be the heroes. They had simply won too much.

Yet, it was noticeable that as UGA marched toward another national championship this season, there was no bad guy looming to prevent it from happening. Saban, the typical antagonist, was nowhere to be found. Two regular-season losses forced the Crimson Tide into a spectator role during the College Football Playoff as the Bulldogs were crowned again.

It's enough to make Georgia fans wonder: If there are no more bad guys standing in the way, does that make the Bulldogs the bad guys now?

Perhaps it does.

If last year saw UGA become the heroes in a feel-good story about claiming a national championship for the first time in decades, then this year might be about establishing the Bulldogs as the permanent villain in every other team's story for having the audacity to come back and win it again. Especially since there's no obvious reason why Georgia would stop hoarding success anytime soon.

Jason Getz

For many fans, that's probably going to take some getting used to.

Last year, folks were happy for you because your favorite team, after enduring an unimaginable drought, finally tasted success. This year they might be jealous of you because your team has decided to hog the spotlight a little too long.

It's all a symptom of head coach Kirby Smart's ambition.

Most of us may have dreamed of one day seeing our favorite teams beat a team such as the Yankees. However, Smart's dream seems to be for UGA to actually be the Yankees, or at least his sport's version of it — a team with a Murderer's Row of talent so deep that it produces a dynasty.

Would anyone doubt his ability to make it happen? Does anyone dispute that it may have already happened?

Last season, Georgia won a national championship by beating Alabama — toppling an empire in the process. This season, the Bulldogs became the sport's new empire.

To those who don't cheer for UGA, it might not exactly be a Hollywood ending. In fact, it may not be an ending at all. It could be just getting started. ∎